RAI

DAYS

Memories of the Delaware Lackawanna and Western Railroad and Erie-Lackawanna Railway Company The Utica Division/Branch

LOUIS C. LANGONE

outskirtspress
DENVER, COLORADO

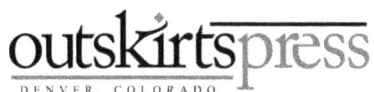

The opinions expressed in this manuscript are solely the opinions of the author and do not represent the opinions or thoughts of the publisher. The author has represented and warranted full ownership and/or legal right to publish all the materials in this book.

Railroad Days
Memories of the Delaware Lackawanna and Western Railroad and Erie-Lackawanna Railway Company The Utica Division/Branch
All Rights Reserved.
Copyright © 2015 Louis C. Langone
v1.0

Cover Image © 2015 Louis C. Langone. All rights reserved – used with permission.

This book may not be reproduced, transmitted, or stored in whole or in part by any means, including graphic, electronic, or mechanical without the express written consent of the publisher except in the case of brief quotations embodied in critical articles and reviews.

Outskirts Press, Inc.
http://www.outskirtspress.com

ISBN: 978-1-4787-0150-7

Library of Congress Control Number 2015931841

Outskirts Press and the "OP" logo are trademarks belonging to Outskirts Press, Inc.

PRINTED IN THE UNITED STATES OF AMERICA

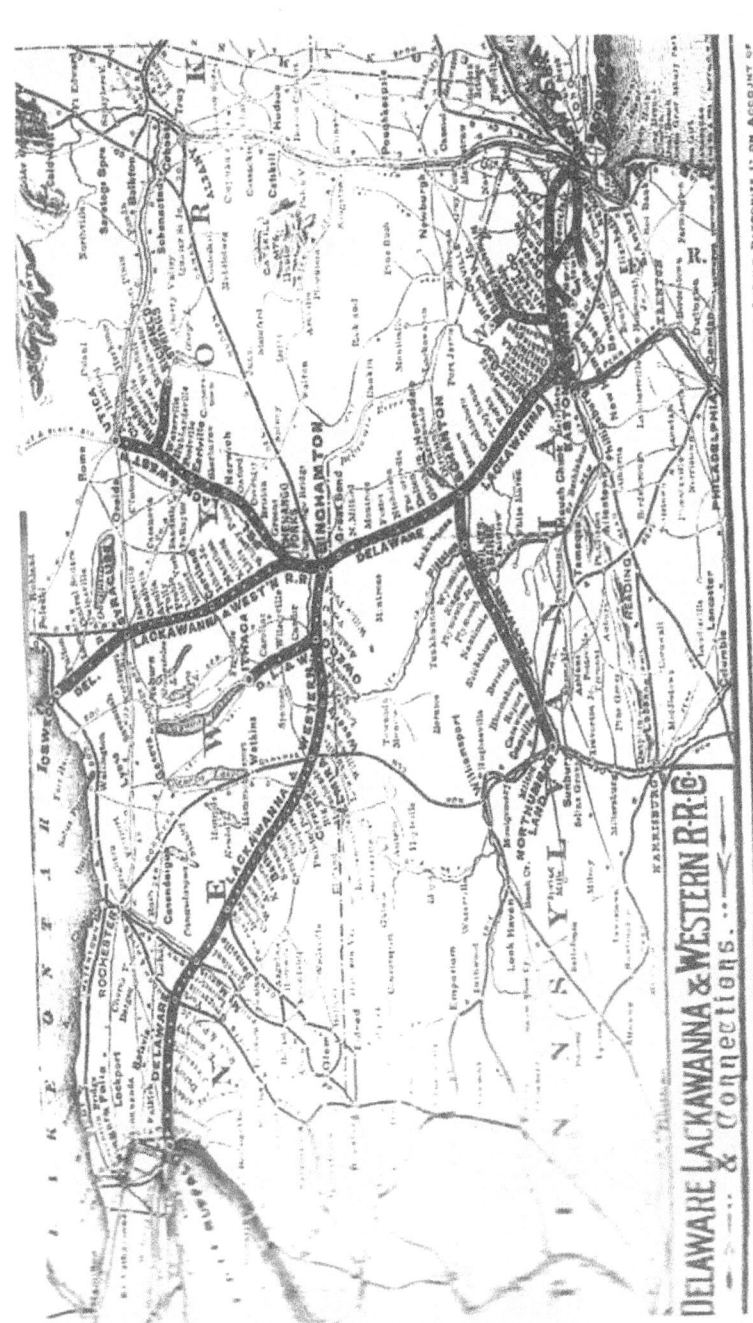

Source: DL&W RR Passenger Timetable

RAILROAD DAYS -

Memories of the
Delaware Lackawanna and Western Railroad
and Erie-Lackawanna Railway Company
The Utica Division/Branch

Louis C. Langone

NOTE FROM THE AUTHOR

Copyright 2006, Louis C. Langone
Revised Edition 2015

No part of this book may be reproduced, stored in a retrieval system, or transmitted by any means, electronic, mechanical, photocopying, recording, or otherwise, without written permission from the author.

For information contact:
Hickory Hill Books
1595 State Route 12
Waterville, NY 13480

E-Mail: loubnc81@gmail.com
Website: www.hickoryhillbooks.com

Front cover artist: Philippa Brown.
Scene from the 1940's. Lincoln-Davies Co., Paris Station. NY

To my wife, Shirlee Tillapaugh Langone for her patience.

To my mother, Catherine Corleto Langone.

To my father - <u>The Company Man -</u>.

To my paternal grandfather, Rocco Langone –the first section foreman

To my oldest brother – Rocco –"Rocky"-the third generation

And, to all the industrious immigrants from the many countries that helped build and maintain the multitude of railroads that crisscrossed the United States of America.

ALSO BY LOUIS C. LANGONE

The Star in the Window-

First Printing.2002
Second Printing-2003
Revised Edition 2011

"Lou's meticulous research offers a much-needed collection of stories about how Central New Yorkers served their country during World War II.

Jack Behrens, Readers' Digest Professor of Magazine author/columnist and host of WIBX/Utica College Roundtable.

<u>The Star in the Window</u> *is a powerful, compelling, and by turns, bittersweet (even, on occasion, amusing) account of the real world of WWII, in the words, and through the eyes, of dozens of Central New York veterans...*

--Richard Searles, Retired English Teacher, Mount Markham Central School, West Winfield, NY.

<u>The Star in the Window</u> *offers a unique view into life during World War II.*

"*I especially enjoyed reading the unusual stories from around the world, i.e., building the Ledo Road in the China-Burma-India Theater of Operations in fighting on the beaches of a Pacific island or manning a gun from a plane over Europe or the Pacific Ocean.....*

Kim Todd, Principal Analyst, ARINC Engineering Services, LLC, Annapolis, MD

ACKNOWLEDGEMENTS

Many people have helped me with <u>Railroad Days</u>. I am grateful to the former railroad employees, their family members, as well as mine, and the many new acquaintances who allowed me to interview them while completing my research.

My thanks to the following who contributed in one way or another regarding the photographs and text that lead to the production of this book:

Philippa Brown, my granddaughter, Brianna Cowen, Doug Ellison, Mary Susan(Fanning)Langone, and Robert Fanning, David Hazelden,, the late Doris Huxtable, Theodore Jackson, Dorothy McConnell, the late John Peterson, "Lester Bugbee, Adele Cooper, Doug Preston, Stan Sambora, Steven Callanen, Fred Lanfear and Sarah Seaman of the Oxford Historical Society, the late Fran Combar, William Szymko, and Harry Lenz of the Utica &Mohawk Valley Chapter of the National Railroad Historical Society. Also, John Taibi (author of several Ontario and Western Railroad books), he late Adrian "Pal" Staring, Jay Winn, the late John Coughlin, Sr.and Jr., the late Bruce Townsend, Max Townsend, the late Betty Townsend, H. Dale Green,, Chenango County Historian Office,

Steve Craig, Chenango County Industrial Development Agency, Pat McKnight of the Steamtown NHS, and Oneida County Historical Society, Waterville Public Library, Waterville Historical Society, Utica Public Library, Mid-York Library, Dana Cross Broedel, Robert Cross, Carolyn Keith, John Huxtable, Lewis Smith, Steve Davis, John Swald, the Lincoln Davies Museum, the Town of Paris Historical Society, Rose Wellman and Town of Sherburne Historical Society, and "Perk" Stalter and the Brookfield Historical Society.

Thanks to the following newspapers: the <u>Waterville Times,</u> and the <u>Utica Observer Dispatch.,</u> <u>The Lackawanna Magazine,</u> and the <u>Syracuse Post Standard</u> for the use of portions of articles and photographs.

Thanks to Patrick Brennan, J. Richard Hughes, the late Lynn Williams and Debra Pugh, Richard Lewis for their information and assistance.

Thanks to my nephew and godson, Louis M. Langone, the fourth generation to work on the Delaware Lackawanna and Western Railroad and Erie-Lackawanna Railway, (summers of 1971 and 1974) for his memorabilia that included my father's copy of <u>Letters to an Old Section Foreman,</u> written by D.E. Gelwix.

A special thank you to Kelly Falk of Waterville, Christopher Langone of Arnold, MD, Jennifer Enos of

Baltimore, MD, and Kim Todd of Annapolis, MD, for their assistance in editing.

Also, the late Walter Rich, CEO of the New York Susquehanna and Western Railway, which still operates today on old DL&W tracks for allowing me to ride on one of his trains, and for answering various questions about the Delaware &Otsego and NYS&W.

Thanks to various employees of the NYS&W RR: Martin Quinn, former Chief of Police, Beth Akulin, Chief Dispatcher, Melanie Boyer, Media Contact person, and van driver Dick Beeman. Thanks to engineer Trent Whitehill and conductor Mark Wilber and retired Utica Yard Conductor, the late George Perrone, who helped acquaint me with locomotive operations, switching of cars and information pertaining to various tracks in the vicinity of the old Utica yard, the Canal Branch, and the old Ontario and Western railroad tracks.

And to the following for assistance with railroad technology: the late Winfred Michel and Robert Masca, Sal Battaglia, Ron Furner, Roger Nichols, Ed Luther, the late Ray Kaminski, James Dundon, Ted Jackson, The late Richard Welch and NYS&W RR Co. employee, Charles Schoenlein.

Most of all, thanks to my son Christopher who once again has assisted me in creating a self-publication.

Evolution of the Delaware Lackawanna and Western Railroad and Four Generations Langone Employees/Section Foreman

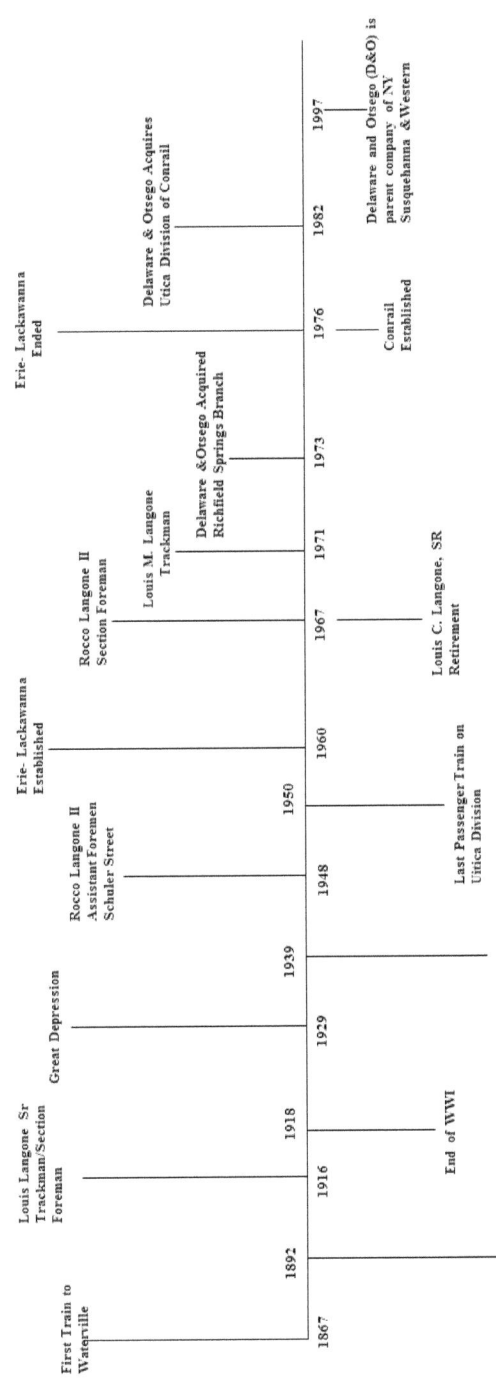

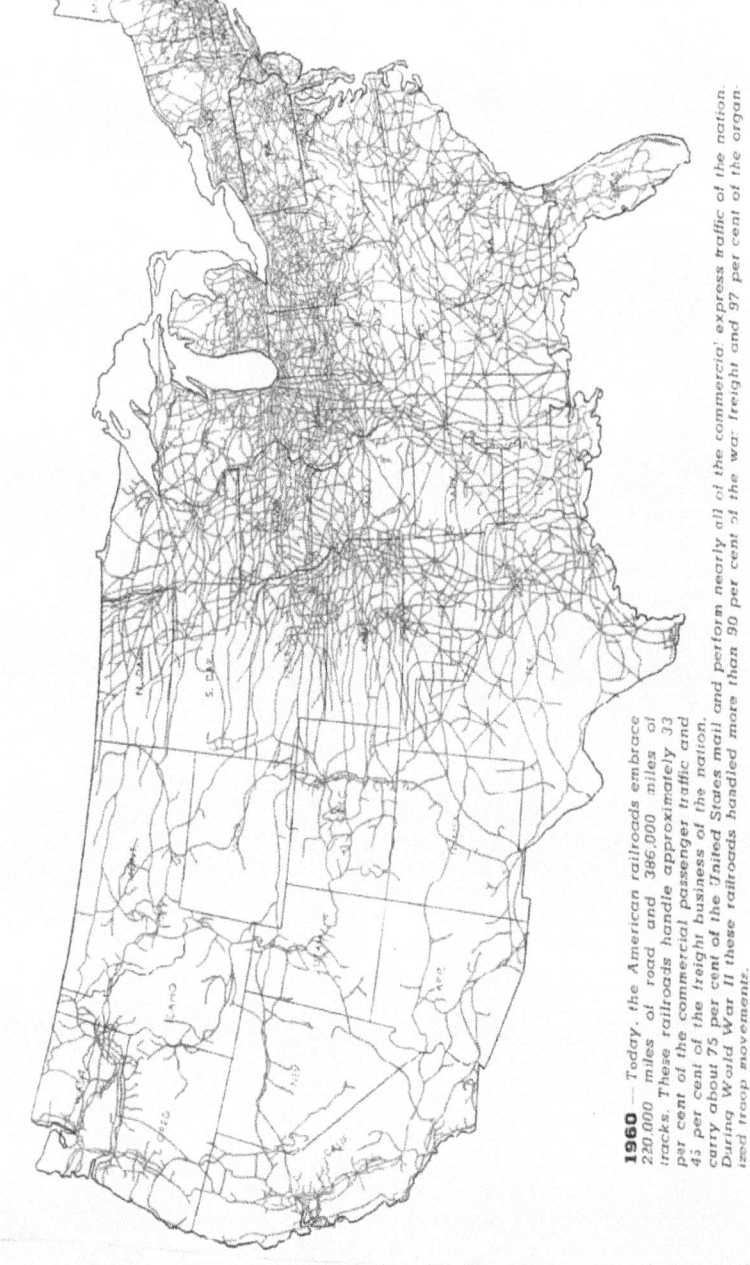

1960—Today, the American railroads embrace 220,000 miles of road and 386,000 miles of tracks. These railroads handle approximately 33 per cent of the commercial passenger traffic and 45 per cent of the freight business of the nation, carry about 75 per cent of the United States mail and perform nearly all of the commercial express traffic of the nation. During World War II these railroads handled more than 90 per cent of the war freight and 97 per cent of the organized troop movements.

South of Loomis Road between Sangerfield and North Brookfield

"A boy's will is the wind's will
    But the thoughts of youth are long, long thoughts."
                    --Henry Wadsworth Longfellow

PREFACE

It is the summer of 2003 and I am standing at Swamp Road grade crossing south of Sangerfield, NY. I am gazing down the tracks at the long cut in the distance toward North Brookfield and the edge of the Nine Mile Swamp where the notorious 19th century Loomis Gang outlaws resided. I think back 60 years ago to 1944 when I was 13 years old and hired to work on the DL&WRR. The extreme summer heat, the vision of the heat waves fluttering over the tracks still linger in my mind. I hear the sounds of steel against steel, the shouting, boisterous laughing, and cursing, hard labor, noon hour poker games and the fun and joking around with all the section hands --working on the railroad.

The boss, my father, the section foreman races up and down the track giving orders—sometimes to a small gang of men – sometimes to a larger one. I see the faces of the diverse groups; the permanent section gang of five or six men, and adding to the regular section, the itinerants – the hoboes of one summer – the Mexicans and the Black migrants of another summer, and in other summers the high school, college students, family members, and just ordinary neighbors of local communities. These railroad regulars and temporary summer time section men along the Utica Branch all made up the human part of an era when the railroad reached its zenith - when ribbons of steel stretched across our nation and was a vital part of nearly every rural and urban community of the country. I can still smell the creosote and hear the sounds of the crunching cinders while working along the track bed. The railroad and the lonesome sound of the steam locomotive whistle linger in my mind while I think of the diminished importance of this mode of transportation in present day America.

The railroad that eventually became known as the Utica Division[1] of the Delaware Lackawanna and Western Railroad existed for more than 100 years about five generations. Four of those five generations had members of the Langone family working that portion of the railroad for 83 years. My close family ties to the railroad once lead a childhood friend to refer to the DL&W as the "Delaware Langone and Western" Railroad.

Few books have been written about the Utica Division, the origins of which date back to the second half of the 19th century. Back then, the DL&W RR was a relatively small railroad, the product of several small lines merged over a period of years. Many railroads have had various nicknames used in jest. The DL&W was referred to as the "Delay, Linger and Wait." The Ontario and Western was the "Old and Weary" and the Delaware and Hudson was the "Dump and Hump." In the book, <u>The Delaware Lackawanna and Western Railroad in the 20th Century, Part I,</u> Thomas Taber includes the following on the title page: "The History and Operation of the Lackawanna Railroad, which would be recognized as mile for mile the most highly developed railroad in America."

During my high school days, I recall a book entitled <u>Clear the Tracks,</u> by Carl Bromley, which related many experiences of

---

[1] According to railroad timetables, the Utica Division extended from Utica, NY to Chenango Forks-a distance of 84.04 miles. Since train traffic extended to Binghamton, the distance between Chenango Forks to Binghamton was sometimes referred to as part of the Utica Division.

iii

the author, a locomotive engineer on the Utica Division of the DL&W RR. The lack of books about the Utica Division[2] has influenced me to write this book relating some stories from members of my family, friends, my own stories, and also stories of anyone who had ever worked on the Utica division of the DL&W RR and the Erie-Lackawanna[3] between 1892 and 1975 until it became a part of the former Conrail. This book pertains to the Maintenance and Way Department of the railroad and this department like the infantry of the army, is not a glamour unit and receives little glory. Books and movies have glorified the operating department- the trains, the engineers and other trainmen as the more romantic segment of railroad folklore. Included in this account is a brief history of the origins of the railroad, select stations along the Utica Division, some companies that had done business with the railroad, railroad terminology, technology, and brief descriptions of some of the railroad occupations. My main source will be my father's stories and my own experiences of having worked on this railroad during several summers of my high school, college, and post-college years. Supplementing these stories will be memories of those outside my family who also worked on the railroad.

---

[2] Utica Division was referred to as a branch of the Scranton Division under the Erie-Lackawanna Railway.
[3] During the years of the Erie-Lackawanna, the Utica Division was referred to as the Utica Branch of the Scranton Division.

It all began with my grandfather, Rocco Langone, the first member of the family to work on the railroad. He emigrated from Italy and after spending some time in South America, returned to Italy and arrived in America a second time and settled in Cassville, New York. He was first employed by the railroad as a track laborer and later became a section foreman. He retired in 1937 after 45 years of service.

Section Foreman, Louis Langone, Sr. and grandson, Robert Langone.1962. The Canal Branch tracks opposite Schultz Body Shop. Route 12 arterial bridge and Schiedelman's Warehouse in distance.

My father, Louis Langone Sr. was born in Cassville and started work at age 14 and also became a section foreman and extra gang section foreman retiring from the Erie-Lackawanna in 1967. My brother, Rocco Langone succeeded my father as section

v

foreman operating out of the railroad yard in Utica and with his section extending south to the Waterville area. He retired in 1980. Other members of my family such as Uncle Fred Julian, some cousins, brothers John, Anthony, Daniel, brother-in-law Winfred Michel, nephews, Louis M. Langone, Salvatore Battaglia, Ron Furner, and Roger Nichols worked in various capacities such as - signal maintainer, ticket agent, section foremen, machinist, equipment operators, or track laborers.

Louis C. Langone, 2014

TABLE OF CONTENTS

CHAPTER	PAGE
INTRODUCTION	1
RAILROAD TECHNOLOGY & OPERATIONS	7
STANDARD TIME	8
RIBBONS OF STEEL	11
THE STEAM LOCOMOTIVE	15
DIESEL LOCOMOTIVE	22
TRAINS ON THE UTICA DIVISION	24
THE CABOOSE	38
PEOPLE AND THE RAILROAD	40
THE TRAINMAN	41
THE SECTION FOREMAN	46
THE RAILROAD WIFE	58
THE TRACKMAN (GRANDY DANCER)	63
THE EXTRA GANG	83
THE TICKET/FREIGHT AGENT	89
THE SIGNAL MAINTAINER	95
THE FARMER AND THE RAILROAD	100
MISCELLANEOUS	108
ACCIDENTS ON RAILROAD CROSSINGS	109
NORTH BROOKFIELD	117

TABLE OF CONTENTS

CHAPTER	PAGE
WORK TRAIN	122
WINTER ON THE RAILROAD	125
RICHFIELD SPRINGS BRANCH	134
THE NINE MILE SWAMP	145
SCHUYLER STREET	149
BUSINESSES ALONG THE DIVISION	159
YE OLDE AMERICAN HOTEL	164
MEMORIES OF SOUTH UTICA	168
EPILOGUE	171
APPENDIX	178
SECTION FOREMAN ROSTER	179
TRACKMAN ROSTER	180
ADDITIONAL PHOTOGAPHS	183
BIBLIOGRAPHY	196
INDEX	200

INTRODUCTION

The Irish and the Welsh built the Delaware Lackawanna and Western Railroad and the Italians, Polish, and other ethnic groups followed in the last decade of the nineteenth century engaging primarily in track work – the Maintenance of Way Department.

The Delaware Lackawanna and Western Railroad was constructed from Scranton, PA to the Delaware River in 1856 and joined to the Central of New Jersey for a route to New York in 1868, the year of my paternal grandfather, Rocco's was born. The DL&W also leased the Morris and Essex Railroad to obtain its own route to the Hudson River and in 1880 the railroad reached Buffalo.

The Lackawanna Railroad wanted to transport coal to central New York and Canada from Pennsylvania. Utica, NY wanted coal to be delivered from Scranton to Utica and this need lead to the construction of the Utica Chenango &Susquehanna RR, which was later leased in 1870 to the DL&W RR for 99 years.

On Thursday, November 14, 1867, in Waterville, ten thousand people celebrated the opening of the railroad between Utica and Waterville. On that day, the town welcomed the first four passenger trains to travel over the Utica, Chenango, and Susquehanna Valley Railroad.[4]

Pat Welch, father of the late Harold Welch of Waterville, traveled from Ireland a year prior to the opening of the railroad, and arrived in the Waterville area by stagecoach.[5] The railroad, which would eventually reach Binghamton and extend on to New York City, provided an advanced transportation alternative to the pre-established horse and stagecoach travel.

The original route plan of the railroad was through the Sauquoit Valley to Cassville, to West Winfield, Richfield Springs, to Cooperstown, Colliersville, Sherburne, Waterville, and back to Utica. However, Cooperstown and Colliersville did not become part of the railroad.

According to the Waterville Times, the building of the railroad from Utica to Cassville was difficult. because of the natural terrain. Tracks had to be built "well up along the side of the mountains, through woods and rocks, and around sharp curves." The 'summit', being the watershed between the source of the Sauquoit and Oriskany Creeks, was reached three and 1/2 miles beyond Cassville.[6] The Waterville Times also mentioned a 100' x 40' building which was erected by George Putnam, to serve as a

---

[4] Waterville Times., Waterville, NY(Date unknown).
[5] Gerry Furner Interview June 10, 2003 and March 20, 2004.
[6] The Waterville Times, (date unknown)

passenger station and storage area. It was three stories high and later used by Buell Boot and the former Waterville Textile Mills.

The first train was made up of seven coaches and a platform car carrying the whole Utica Fire Department as well as 100 military personnel and stopped at Waterville at 11:35 a.m. where the whistles of the four engines blew their longest and shrillest shrieks. "The cannons roared their loudest notes, awakening reverberations never before disturbed among the hills of Waterville," the Waterville Times recorded.

By 1868, the tracks were completed to Sherburne and the first official train arrived at Sherburne August 8 of that year. My grandfather, who began his employment with the railroad in 1892, was almost four months old at this time.

The Norwich Telegraph reported that, "There were seven trains drawing 56 cars. – Two trains from Waterville with five bands. There was one train from Washington Mills with three bands and four trains from Utica."[7]

The first train from Utica to Norwich ran October 6, 1869. "It carried twelve cars filled with Knights Templar of the Masonic Lodges of Utica and Waterville."[8]

---

[7] Thomas T. Taber III, The Delaware Lackawanna and Western Railroad In The Nineteenth century., p. 241.
[8] Ibid., p.246.

By 1870 passenger trains were operating between Utica and Binghamton. And by November 25, 1872, work was completed on the Richfield Junction to the Richfield Springs branch.[9]

It was in 1880 that the railroad introduced the symbol signifying locomotives burning the cleaner anthracite blue coal rather than bituminous coal, for fuel. "Stay white from morn to night upon the Road of Anthracite[10] The symbol, became known as Phoebe Snow – portrayed as a young woman whose gown was white.

I first heard about Phoebe Snow from my father who would recite a verse or two from the poem... The poem tells the story of Phoebe Snow, who dressed in white and whose dress remained untainted while traveling the "Road of Anthracite." The symbol and poem turned out to be great advertising for the railroad. Phoebe was a mythical character from Lackawanna railroad folklore who, I, of course, would never meet, but she would always remain in my memory.

During World War I, the government prohibited the use of anthracite coal in steam locomotives, since anthracite coal was in demand for heating purposes.

---

[9] Ibid. p. 246.
[10] George H. Drury, The Train-Watchers Guide to North American Railroads. Milwaukee, WI, 1984, p. 67.

After 1920, however, anthracite coal could not be used for the newer locomotives so the dirtier soft bituminous coal replaced

the hard anthracite. However, for advertising purposes, the railroad still referred to itself as "The Route of Phoebe Snow."[11]

The railroads of America played a significant role during both of the World Wars of the 20th century. However, a far more important role was played by the railroads during World War II. During World War I the government took over the railroads and they operated at a loss costing the taxpayer $2,000,000 a day. In

---

[11] Robert Hutchinson, Steamtown Historic Site presentation, .August 23, 2004.

World War II the owners kept control of the railroads and it contributed more than $3,000,000 a day in taxes. During World War II, "97% of all troops and 90% of all Army and Navy equipment was transported by rail. All of this was due to several factors such as improved technology, careful planning, and the loyal efforts of railway employees- trainmen, freight and station agents, and trackmen."[12]

---

[12] American Railroads-Their Growth and Development., Association of American Railroads, pp.31-32.

RAILROAD OPERATIONS AND TECHNOLOGY

The Hamilton Watch – "the watch of railroad accuracy," according to an old radio commercial. The exact watch that was carried by section foreman, Louis Langone, Sr... Courtesy of Eugene and Tim Langone. Photograph by Tim Langone.

STANDARD TIME

Whenever railroaders get together, the topic of standard time seems to enter the conversation. This book would not be complete without brief mention of this concept.

RAILROAD DAYS

My grandfather, father, and brother Rocco, always owned a Hamilton gold pocket watch. As the Hamilton radio advertisements used to say – "the watch of railroad accuracy." My brother, Anthony, who worked as a signal maintainer, wore an Elgin wrist-watch, and also had to have it inspected periodically. Their watches were always set on standard time- -or as we part-time railroad workers used to say--"railroad time."

Because of the lack of a standard time, confusion ran prevalent in railroad operations. "A traveler from Maine to California, in order to have correct railroad time, had to change his watch some twenty times during the journey. When it was noon in Chicago it was 12:31 in Pittsburgh; 12:24 in Cleveland; 12:17 in Toledo; 12:13 in Cincinnati." Each city kept the local time of its own meridian and true "sun time" was not observed.[13]

Consequently, the Association of American Railroads and its predecessors helped to put the railroads on standard time by November 18, 1883 and four United States time zones were established... Prior to that date, each railroad ran its trains by the local time of one or more of the cities on the line and at one time, there were "68 different local times by which the trains were operated."[14]

---

[13] "The Day of Two Noons," http://.fremo.org/betreib/timezone.htm.p.2.
[14] American Railroads, Their Growth and Development. The Association of American Railroads, p.22

This date, November 18, was called "the day of two noons." "In the eastern part of each time zone there was a noon based upon sun-time; then clocks and watches were set back from one to thirty minutes to the new standard time, so that there was another noon when standard time in the community reached 12:00 o'clock."[15] An international conference in 1884 led to a worldwide system of twenty-four time zones. The time zone kept in each zone is based on the central meridian at 15° intervals.[16] In the United States, federal legislation did not come until 1918 when Congress passed the Standard Time Act.[17]

---

[15] "The Day of Two Noons," op.cit. p.2
[16] World Book Encyclopedia, Vol.18, p.655 1973.
[17] American Railroads, Their Growth and Development. The Association of American Railroads, p. 22.

Scene is south of Lewis crossing-about two miles north of Waterville

RIBBONS OF STEEL

When the railroads of America were built, the rails on which the trains ran, differed in composition and size. Rails making up the first tracks were made of wood and topped with metal strips of iron to make the rails more durable. Iron rails replaced the wooden ones and weighed 50 to 56 pounds to the yard. In 1865 the railroads began to use rails made from steel. The length of the rail also varied over the years. In 1920 the standard length of the rail was 33 feet and this was the length usually used on the Utica branch. In1960 rail length on many railroads had increased to 39 feet and some of the railroads used 60 to 78 foot rails.

Rail size also depended where on the line it was located. The branch lines had smaller size, compared to the main line. The main line of the DL&W RR, which had heavier passenger and freight traffic, was double track and ran from Hoboken, NJ to Buffalo, NY. On the Utica Branch, the size was 80 lb. to the yard until the larger rail- 105 lb. to the yard -was laid during World War II. The Richfield Junction to Richfield Springs spur or branch-line of the Utica Division had even smaller rail – 75 lb. to the yard. Also, on this route, screw spikes rather than cut spikes were used. The older style screw spikes had to be screwed into the railroad tie with a screw type wrench operated usually by one man.

When this author first started working on the railroad, the section gangs doubled up for a rail-laying job in the vicinity of Greene, NY. The smaller 80 lb. to a yard rail was being replaced with 105 lb. to the yard. The rail length was usually 33 feet. The old rails were knocked off the ties and larger plates for the 105 lb. rail were substituted. The old spikes were for the most part, the smaller size cut spikes.

For most of the railroad's era, a slight gap between the rails usually existed. Many abutted one another. This can be a problem during extreme summer heat which causes the steel to expand. As the rails tightened, the tracks would sometimes buckle into an S shape. Over the years, I have traveled countless miles by rail. Click-clack, click-clack, was the all-familiar sound as the train passed over the rail joints and that sound increased as one passed from one coach to another. The joints on both sides of the tracks were seldom, if ever, opposite one another.

"Continuous" rail involved welding the joints together for a mile or more [18] I recall welding gangs of the 1940's fusing rails together. "It did not buckle from the heat because the track structure resisted the thermal expansion and contraction and the elasticity of the steel, forces dimensional changes to occur in the cross-section of the rail rather than in its length."[19] As an interesting side-note; the longest continuous welded rail in the United States in 1958 was 33,792 feet. Many stretches of continuous rail are more than a mile in length.[20]

Ron Furner, my nephew by marriage, worked on the Utica Division before moving to Warners, NY. When he worked on the Utica Division, he was a mechanic and had also worked in the DL&W RR roundhouse in the Utica Yard. There he cleaned and oiled the locomotives. Furner added the following about Continuous Welded Rail:

---

[18] American Railroads, Their Growth and Development. The Association of American Railroads p.25
[19] Richard Reinhardt, Workin' On the Railroad, Palo Alto, American West Publishing Co, 1970.
[20] Ibid., p. 25

...Continuous welded rail (CWR) today is about one-quarter mile in length sections. When it is laid the temperature has to be taken. The temperature has to be 90° and it is anchored down with rail anchors (creepers). This eliminates the expansion that would normally occur because of the summer heat. In colder weather, especially around 0°, contraction occurs and joints open and resulting pressure causes rails to break creating loud snapping noises. At railroad crossings hi-density rail is used to avoid contraction from cold weather.

The late Bruce Townsend, who had been employed by the Erie-Lackawanna and CSX, had pointed out to the author that there had been times in the winter when large gaps occurred at the joints, and it became necessary to place rope and/or sawdust on the rails and then ignite rope or sawdust to reduce the contraction.

On a recent trip on AMTRAK, it sounded to me that the once familiar uneven click-clack, click-clack, click-clack sound of the train passing over the joints has been greatly eliminated by the welding of the rail joints. I also noticed that the diesel-electric locomotive was equipped with the old style whistle. Perhaps, some of the romantic railroad past has, once again, reappeared on the scene.

1200 Steam Locomotive- 2-8-2. Used on the Utica Division in the 1940's.

THE STEAM LOCOMOTIVE

"I can hear yet the mid-night whistle of the train as it went through North Brookfield…" *Mary Raffauf Lillie*

There are few wonders in the world of transportation capturing the imagination more than the steam locomotive projecting its lonesome sound of the whistle and the unique engine noises as it traveled through the valleys, over the plains, hills, and mountains of America. A wide variety of models and sizes hauled the passenger and freight trains in the 19th century and over 50 years of the 20th century. More than 40,000 steam engines were built between 1829 and 1949. Most were retired in the 1960's.

The wheel arrangements of a steam locomotive (2-6-2, 4-4-0, or 4-8-8-4 types), for example, is explained as follows: The first figure of the arrangement refers to the number of leading wheels, the last is the number of trailing wheels and the middle figures (or numbers) give the number and arrangement of the drivers.

Throughout the years of the DL&W, a variety of steam locomotives were in operation. During the early years the 4-4-0 type was most commonly used on freight and passenger trains. Later the 2-6-0 and 2-8-0 were used on freight trains.[21]

The Lackawanna was one of the anthracite railroads and also owned anthracite mines in Pennsylvania. Anthracite is a hard coal that burns slowly with little smoke and was used for home heating. A fine material had to be removed from the anthracite and was a waste product known as culm. However, it did not burn well in the long narrow fireboxes. It was necessary to use a wider grate. In 1877, John E. Wooten, a railroad superintendent, designed a boiler that would burn the smaller sized anthracite.[22] The new firebox required it to be placed above the driving wheels. So the

---

[21] Sheldon S. King, The Route of Phoebe Snow., p.119.
[22] http://www..steamlocomotive.com/camelback/, p.1

RAILROAD DAYS 17

engineer's cab[23] was moved ahead of the firebox astride the boiler and the fireman remained in the rear. This resulted in what became known as the Camelback or Mother Hubbard type of locomotive. "The DL&W used the camelback engine into the 20th century and was an ideal passenger locomotive because the hard coal burned almost without smoke."[24]

The "Mother Hubbard" was more dangerous for the fireman and the engineer. For example, the fireman had to stand on a moving platform while stoking the boiler and the engineer sat over a "whirling drive rod and had no way to escape should a rod break." It was phased out in 1927 by the Interstate Commerce Commission.[25]

The "Pacific" 4-6-2 type was also used by the Lackawanna. The "Pacific" was the main steam passenger locomotive during the first 50 years of the 20th century.[26] Built by ALCO, the K class had 79-inch drivers, 185 psi, and a starting tractive effort of 40,800 pounds. The grate was 59.7 square feet.[27]

Horsepower and tractive effort together determine the movement of trains and the type of locomotive needed. A certain amount of tractive force is needed to start a train and to move up grades. The weight of the locomotive on the wheels must be of a

---

[23] The engineer sits in right side of the locomotive cab.
[24] Ibid., p.2.
[25] Ibid., p.2.
[26] http://www.steamlocomotive.com/pacific, p.1.
[27] Ibid., p. 2.

certain amount to start a pull. Horsepower moves a train at a certain speed.[28]

The steam locomotive required much maintenance and often had mechanical problems. Robert Hutchinson, a locomotive engineer and volunteer, at the Steamtown Railroad Museum in Scranton, PA, explained how it requires eight hours to get a steam locomotive ready for service and once a day, the engine must drop its ashes.

William Doyle, a resident of Waterville said that he remembered the steam engines breaking down once in a while. After breaking down, they would park on the sidetrack near the hop warehouse that located between Putnam and White Streets and near Benedict and Doolittle Place.".

Cattle on the track sometimes derailed early locomotives. To avoid these derailments, a device known, as the cowcatcher was devised that was attached to the front of the locomotive.

The origins of the cowcatcher can be traced to the mid-nineteenth century mechanical engineer who designed spikes to be placed on either side of the engine. However, this was considered quite cruel to the cows. A V-shaped structure was designed and was found to be quite effective. Unfortunately, it did not prevent cows that got on the tracks from being injured .

---

[28] John H. Armstrong, The Railroad-What It Is, What It Does, p. 41Omaha: Simmons-Boardman Publishing Corp., 1977.

RAILROAD DAYS 19

. Locomotive- No. 948. Type 4-4-0 – 1911 vintage. Photo by Hazen Hinman, Jr., Utica, NY. 1934., Files of Utica & Mohawk Valley NRHS.

Locomotive – No. 964-Type: 4-4-0 – 1903 vintage. Photo by Hazen Hinman, Jr... 1937. Files of Utica &Mohawk Valley Chapter NRHS. Watchman's tower still adorns East Main Street in Norwich, NY.

2300 Steam Locomotive – Steamtown National Historic Museum. Scranton, PA. 2002. Photo by David Hazelden.

Diesel Locomotive and freight train – Binghamton. Photograph by Jay Winn

RAILROAD DAYS 21

Waiting for a ride on a diesel locomotive in 1962. Near Shultz Body Shop and Schiedelman Warehouse. Trainman-George Ellis. Section Foreman Louis Langone, Sr. and grandson, Robert Langone.

Inside the cab of NYS&W Railway Co. diesel locomotive.

Erie-Lackawanna 2585Diesel Locomotive. Trainman John Swald is in the cab on the right Files of John Swald. Photo by Jim Muller

DIESEL LOCOMOTIVE

The invention of the diesel engine was a major advancement, in power and efficiency, for railroad transportation. The power plant of the diesel-electric locomotive was made up of the engine and the generator or alternator "which converted the crankshaft motion into electrical energy for traction."[29] The diesel locomotives have tremendous power and require less manpower to maintain compared with the steam locomotive. The railroad introduced the diesel for the first time on the Utica division in 1951. In the1960's and 1970's, the EMD-General Motor diesels

---

[29] John H. Armstrong, The Railroad, What It Is, What It Does. P. 52

were operating on the Utica Division. "They were mainly of the 1200 type."[30] Numerous water tanks that provided the necessary water for the steam engines were familiar sights along the railroad. These were no longer required and were all eventually torn down. Climbing Paris Hill became less of a problem for the diesel powered freight trains. It was not too long before the fireman, who no longer had to shovel coal for the boiler, was being thought of as an unnecessary crewmember. The Brotherhood of Trainmen Union, who fought to keep the fireman as a crewmember, was accused of promoting "featherbedding." (Retention of unnecessary personnel in employment)

---

[30] John Swald Interview, January 22, 2005.

R. R. Depot, Waterville, N.Y.

Passenger train arriving at Waterville station in late 19th or early 20th century. Courtesy of Waterville Historical Society.

TRAINS ON THE UTICA DIVISION

There were passenger train station stops located at practically every community, village or hamlet between Utica and Binghamton and on the smaller branch from Richfield Junction at Cassville to Richfield Springs.

The last passenger train to travel the Utica Division was in April of 1950. The following is an old passenger train announcement of the schedule that is still posted today at the Lincoln Davis museum at Paris Station, New York:

RAILROAD DAYS

NOTICE

EFFECTIVE OCTOBER 29TH, AND THEREAFTER, TRAINS NO. 1803 AND 1816 WILL OPERATE UNDER THE FOLLOWING SCHEDULE:

Read Down 1803 Daily	Stations	Read Up 1816 Daily
2:45 P.M.	Lv. Binghamton	Ar. 8:00 P.M
f 2:55 P.M.	Lv. Chenango Bridge	Ar. 7:43 P.M.
3:03 P.M.	Lv. Chenango Forks	Ar. 7:35 PM
3:14 P.M.	Lv. Greene	Ar. 7:23 P.M.
----------	Brisbane	----------
---------	Lv. Coventry	f Ar 7:06 P.M.
3:34 P.M.	Lv. Oxford	Ar. 6:59 P.M.
f 3:51 P.M.	Lv. Norwich	Ar. 6:46 P.M.
3:59 P.M.	Lv Galena	f Ar. 6:34 P.M.
4:07 P.M.	Lv. Sherburne	Ar. 6:25 P.M.
4:15 P.M.	Lv. Earlville	Ar. 6:16 P.M.
4:21 P.M.	Lv. Poolville	Ar. 6:11 P.M.
4:28 P.M.	Lv. Hubbardsville	Ar. 6:04 P.M
4:34 P.M.	Lv. North Brookfield	Ar. 5:58 P.M.
f 4:44 P.M.	Lv. Waterville	Ar. 5:48 P.M.
f 4:50 P.M.	Lv. Paris	Ar. 5:40 P.M>
4:58 P.M.	Lv. Richfield Junction	Ar. 5:31 P.M.
f 5:02 P.M.	Lv. Clayville	Ar. 5:21 P.M
5:05 P.M.	Lv. Sauquoit	Ar. 5:16 P.M.
5:12 P.M.	Lv. Chadwicks	Ar. 5:12 P.M.
5:20 P.M.	Lv. New Hartford	Ar. 5:05 P.M.
5:35 P.M.	Ar. Utica	Lv. 4:50 P.M.

LACKAWANNA

During the Depression, quite a few trains still ran. In the 1930's there were six to eight trains every day- including four passenger trains. The "Hot Shot" was a fast freight made up of 25-30 cars. The "Bull" was a slower freight of about 40-50 cars that traveled at night and picked up only the empty cars. The "Bull" was listed on the board schedule as BU1(The BU referring to Binghamton to Utica).[31] Jay Winn of New Hartford feels that the "Bull" got its name from the fact that it was listed on the board as BU11. There was also the "Extra" at night that did pick up freight.[32]

The "Local" went every other day from Utica to Norwich and returned the next day with freight to Utica. A "Local" train also ran from Binghamton to Norwich every other day.[33]

Before World War II the locomotive sizes were 300's, and 700's (numerals shown on the front of the locomotives) that hauled freight. The largest engines on the Utica Branch, the 1200's, that pulled passenger trains were used around World War II. Sometimes the 2100's ran on the Utica Division. During the war the government ran army engines. Heavier, they caused some concern as to whether the bridges could withstand the weight of these huge locomotives. These were used to haul freight. The

---

[31] George Perrone Interview. January 11, 2005.
[32] Louis C. Langone, Sr.- Audiocassette-1977
[33] Theodore Jackson, Personal Interview, July 7, 2004.

troop trains used 1200 engines. Sometimes they were double-headers.[34]

Perrone also recalled that the freight train in the Utica Yard moved paper goods to the Sitroux Plant. Cars were brought to the Team Track (designated siding used to hold railroad cars for later pick-up) in New Hartford and then the "Hot Shot" would take them to Binghamton and meet with a freight train on the main line (Buffalo, NY to Hoboken, NJ).[35]

Prior to the arrival of the diesel on the Utica Branch, freight trains going north through Waterville often had difficulty cresting Paris Hill. Leaving Waterville, it is all up hill to the summit at Paris Station located in the area of the Lincoln-Davies lumber yard. Leaving Waterville, the steam locomotive chugged and puffed and dropped sand on the ball of the rail for traction. The wheels of the locomotive would spin and create burn spots on the top of the rail. Sometimes the train went as far as it could- perhaps the curve at Cobblestone Road, just south of Summit Road crossing.[36] If the train couldn't make the first curve, it would leave one-half of the train on the main track temporarily. Reaching Paris Station, the front half was left temporarily in the passing siding. The locomotive would leave from the front end of the passing siding and then double back in reverse to hook onto the

---

[34] George Perrone Interview- May 18, 2004
[35] Ibid.
[36] Louis Langone, Sr., Interview, Audiocassette, 1977.

rest of the train. Other times the locomotive left one-half of the train on the passing side in Waterville and the front half would go on to Paris Station and then double back. Splitting the train in each of these two ways has often been referred to as "doubling the hill." "The passing siding at Paris Station passed over the crest or summit of Paris Hill and was lower than the main track. Sometimes when we approached the summit and because of the concern about the excess tonnage on the front end of the train, the headman on the front of the engine would run ahead of the train to throw the switch lining the main track with the siding. Half of the train was uncoupled and it would head down the grade to the passing siding. This would avoid a double cut." Perrone explained.[37]

When special trains such as troop trains ran south from Utica, there was difficulty making the hill to Paris Station. Half of the train was left at Washington Mills and half taken to the siding at Paris and then the engine would return for the other half.

My nephew, Louis M. Langone, recalled a story about the steep grade from Cassville south to Paris Station:

...Years ago (when I worked for the Town of Marshall Highway Department), a co-worker and I were checking roads. When we drove over the Summit Road crossing where the Renkin (Marshall) milk plant had been located, we talked about that milk plant and the many other milk stations that were once located along the railroads in the area. He told me a story about when he

---

[37] George Perrone Interview, April 1, 2005.

was a young boy in Cassville. He said he and a couple of his buddies would walk up to the Cassville junction (Richfield Junction) and they would take bars of lye soap with them. They would then rub soap on the rails on both sides of the track from the Junction toward Paris. From the Junction south to Paris, the grade is quite steep and it was a hard pull for the steam engines. When the next steam engine came along from the Junction with a full head of steam it would hit the area where the boys had done their prank and the wheels of the engine immediately began to spin and the engine would lose its momentum until it could not go any further. At that time the engineer would let out a blast from the whistle and then begin backing up to try the grade again. Sometimes it would take a few times before all the lye soap was worn off the tracks. Needless to say the poor fireman stoking the steam engine did not see the same humor in the prank that the boys did.

There were seventeen stations with passing sidings between Chenango Forks and Utica and two on the smaller Richfield Branch." The car capacity plus the engine and caboose of some of the sidings are as follows: Paris Station - 100 cars. North Brookfield - 48 cars, Sherburne – 82, and Waterville – 62.[38] Back in the 1930's and 1940's, railroad cars were only about 40 feet long. Hopper cars that carried coal were less than forty feet. In the late 1950's car lengths extended to seventy feet and the western railroads had even longer freight cars. Box cars were about fifty feet long and flat cars about eighty-nine feet.[39]

---

[38] The DL&WRR Co. Timetable No.76, p. 28, 1938.
[39] Theodore Jackson, op. cit., JULY 7, 2004.

The late Robert Masca, a former trackman and section foreman, said that prior to Conrail, there was a local, a freight train that went from Utica to Sangerfield on certain days. – It also ran from Utica to Richfield Springs on another day. Masca described the "Bull" as a freight train that ran from Utica to Binghamton to Scranton, PA. He said those were the days when a trainman could work 16 hours straight. Later they were limited to eight hours.[40]

Masca, thinking about one of the memorable events of his career on the railroad, also recalled an accident that occurred in Clayville when the train crew was switching railroad cars. "The crew had set one of the cars on the main line, put the brake on and went back to the siding. The brakeman noticed that the car began to roll so he jumped on the car and tried to set the brake but could not stop the car. He rode the car all the way to Higby Road and then jumped before the car struck an automobile and dragged it down the tracks killing the auto's driver. In the accident, the brakeman also had some injuries.

Roger Nichols, my nephew and a former section hand and equipment operator for the Erie-Lackawanna RR, relates a story emphasizing the importance of knowing the exact whereabouts of trains on the line and obtaining train lineups (schedule of trains) from the dispatcher. In this way, the section foreman can keep tabs on the trains when working on the tracks.

---

[40] Robert Masca, January 20, 2004.

RAILROAD DAYS   31

Recalling a day in 1973 or 1974, Nichols says.

It was a typical Friday patrol day. The gang was notified to go to the Marshall crossing north of Waterville. Some of Martin's (farm on Summit Road) cows had wandered onto the tracks and the fence had to be repaired. Cell phones were a convenience of the future and the Western Union lines were no longer in operation along the tracks. Consequently, the section foreman had no portable phone to hook on to these lines to use to communicate with the dispatcher in Utica or Binghamton. At the Yard Office in Utica, Rocky, [41] the section foreman, would normally tell the engineer, Ray Kaminski,[42] of the "local" freight train heading for Binghamton. to look out for us since we would be fixing fence at Marshall crossing... However, this time we didn't tell the engineer, but on our way we left torpedoes on the rail to alert the engineer of us working ahead of the train.

We left for Marshall and Rocky was driving. Dick Welch, Jerry Massago, and two black men, Clarence and Mike, who had recently been hired rode from Utica on the high railer.[43] We arrived at the Marshall crossing area and proceeded to repair fence. We had a roll of fence and when that ran out we used old Western Union wire.

We didn't hear the freight train approaching.[44] We should have heard the whistle since there are lots of crossings where the whistle is blown, but the noise from Martin's grain elevator must have drowned out the sound of the whistle.

We were loading up and ready to go home and we had just got back to the truck. The 1963 International high railer was notorious for stalling, and there were many miles on it. I had said to Clarence and Mike –'If you see the train coming, let us know.' They were

---

[41] Rocco Langone-author's brother.
[42] Ray was a diesel-electric locomotive engineer. engineer and worked for over 30 years with the DL&W and the Erie-Lackawanna
[43] Truck like vehicle that operates on the track.
[44] Diesels are not as noisy as a steam locomotive.

riding in the back. I don't think the truck was yet in third gear when we heard Clarence and Mike rapping on the rear of the truck. I looked in the rear view mirror and the train was so close I couldn't even see the headlight. The speed limit was 40 MPH for the train. That was close! So we take off and Rocky is driving. How he hit the gears I don't know and he finally got the truck up to 60 miles an hour. The engineer, Kaminski, threw on the emergency brake and as steel made contact with steel the locomotive and cars were sliding down the tracks, since it takes a long distance to stop. When we first noticed the train we were barely moving. If we had spent another five minutes fixing the fence, the train would have had the truck.

Dick Baldwin, a farm owner north of Waterville, told Nichols later that he was looking east from his farm toward the tracks. He witnessed the scene and wondered what was going on with the high railer speeding down the tracks with a freight train in pursuit. "It was the funniest thing I ever saw," Baldwin remarked. "The truck was flying down the track with the train chasing it and all I saw was a cloud of dust. The cloud of dust was from Cobblestone crossing (Lewis Road), a dirt crossing." Nichols said that after about a mile they reached Putnam Street crossing in Waterville and took the high-railer truck off the tracks. "Needless to say," Nichols said, "Rocky and the conductor, Junior Conklin, had some words. Thinking back, it seems kind of funny," Nichols added with a laugh. "Fortunately, an accident was avoided."

Dick Welch who worked on the section from 1971-76 recalled the following about the incident:

…We were fixing fence and "Rocky" said there would be no train for a while since it was assumed that it would be doing switching work at the Junction.[45]

…We finished fixing the fence and Rocky sent me down to bring up the high railer. Rocky was driving and before long we discovered the train coming. It came earlier than expected, since that day there was no switching at the Junction... We were going about 60 miles an hour going by Cobblestone Crossing and we had thoughts of jumping and the doors were open and slamming back and forth. Gene Trepezea was the fireman and I found out later Gene had thrown the emergency brake. I think that Dick O'Hare was the engineer and not Ray Kaminski. Dick Baldwin was cutting hay at the time and saw us racing the train to Waterville.

The ICC(Interstate Commerce Commission) has reported that many lives have been lost and many injuries have occurred from section-car or motor car .accidents with trains.. The section-cars have sometimes been called "pop cars" or speeders. I have never heard them referred to as a "pop car" or speeder.

Trains have also presented a potential hazard to non-employees who walked the railroad tracks. Though the approaching steam locomotive could be heard for long distances, pedestrian fatalities did occur. Ronald Jones, proprietor of Lincoln-Davies of Paris Station, NY related a story that his mother had written in her diary. He said that his mother had written in her diary that three Lincoln-Davis farm employees had been drinking and were struck by a train between Cassville and Paris. "They had

---

[45] Richfield Junction at Cassville where the Utica Division is joined by the Richfield Springs Branch

gotten drunk in Cassville and probably sat on the rails to rest and fell asleep and a big freight cut up the heads of all three. The section men in the morn (sic) left them in the depot," Mrs. Jones recorded in her diary. She also described a later incident when she found a shoe in the snow while walking to ride the train to school from Paris Station. "To my horror it had a foot inside. There was blood in the snow and when I reached the station I heard there was a body in the freight house. Hoboes traveled that way on the railroad. If I remember right they never knew where this man came from," she wrote. For many years, the transportation of U.S. Mail was an important function of the railroads. The late Worth Warner of North Brookfield, NY said that in the 1940's, there were two passenger trains in the morning each way and two in the evening each way. There was also the "Extra" that picked up freight at night. The passenger trains would have a mail and express car that transported mail and express until passenger train service. Martin Cleary of Waterville said that when he was in college at Holy Cross that Roger Kane would pick up mail in the morning and deliver it to the railroad station. It would arrive in Worcester, MA, a distance of over 150 miles, that same night.

The late Jack Gallagher, who lived all of his life in Sangerfield recalled the passenger trains carrying the mail. When he was a young boy, he would walk down to the tracks and watch the mail arrive. The following is Gallagher's observation of one of the mail arrivals:

RAILROAD DAYS

...John Heckert was the postmaster in Sangerfield, and in the winter Heckert wore a long bearskin coat to his ankles and he would use a sled to pick up the mail. About 150 yards below the old Route 20 intersection, there was an arm constructed on a post for the mail. Since the train didn't stop at Sangerfield, the guy in the mail car would reach out with the mail bag so the arm would catch it... Once in a while he would miss and Heckert would have to go down the track in search of the mail bag. In the winter the bag sometimes landed in the snow and John would go down to try and find the mail.

Gallagher also remembers a building for livestock between Putnam and White Streets on the East side of the tracks, where livestock would be loaded aboard cattle cars. He also said that in Sangerfield about two hundred yards north of the underpass adjacent to William Chernoff's farm, there was an old milk station that later became a farmer co-op bean vinery. There was also a former ice house where the Gallaghers stored hay. Gallagher took the horses up to the fence and their heads close to the tracks while the hay was being loaded or unloaded. "I would drive up pretty close to the tracks and when the horses heard the engine blow the whistle for the White Street crossing or see the steam from the locomotive. They would get a little more difficult to control. However, the team was pretty used to the whistle."

Gallagher said that the trestle on the Route 12 portion of the railroad line probably was constructed in the early 1920's. Sangerfield was not a regular stop for passenger trains but the railroad allowed the train to be flagged so passenger could get aboard and their fare would be collected by the conductor. "One time, my mother flagged the train and we rode the train to Binghamton and then to Bath, NY," Gallagher added.

For various reasons, derailments sometimes occurred leading to severe injury or death. One memorable derailment occurred in Bridgewater in early 1942. A freight train approached Bridgewater crossing one day and ran through an open switch which spread the switch point. The train, with a light locomotive, passed over it without incident but this still left a potential hazard to trains that followed, if the damage done to the switch was not repaired.

In a recorded conversation with my father, Louis Langone, Sr, he described how the derailment occurred.

...When the train that had run through the switch then arrived at Richfield Junction, the conductor informed the dispatcher instead of reporting it to the section foreman, Fred Julian. The following morning, the "Local" (freight train) came through to do some work before going on to Richfield Springs. When it got to Bridgewater, Junior Mack, the engineer, maintained speed traveling along at thirty miles an hour and went through that same switch with the spread switch point. The engine went on the ground onto its side. Mack was thrown out on his back. He lived for a while but later died as a result of the accident. What caused the accident? The dispatcher in Binghamton should have held the train, the "Local," from going to Richfield Springs and the conductor of the first train should have notified the section foreman to check out and repair the switch.[46]

---

[46] Louis C. Langone, Audiocassette- 1977.

George Perrone also remembered this accident.

. ... It occurred on the north end of the Bridgewater siding. The engine was on its side. After the first train spread the points, it was not reported right by the conductor. He should have reported it the following way: 'The switch has been run through and cannot be used.' "The switch should have been spiked so it can't be used. The conductor didn't say that the points had been opened and had not been repaired. My dad used to say that if you can put your fist between the stock rail[47] and the point at the end- it would be ok." (for a train to go over it) [48]

The gang worked all day and night and all of the next day to repair the track and the former hotel on the southwest corner of Routes 8 and 20 at Bridgewater made sandwiches for the men. Working continuously for forty hours, the men had trouble staying awake.

It was the last day that the writer's brother, Rocco, worked before being drafted into the Army.

---

[47] Stock Rail- Special point-shaped section of rail that lines main track to sidetrack.
[48] George Perrone Interview, May 18, 2004

Tail end of the "Bull" (BU1)-Utica-1969. This freight train with caboose and boxcar, illustrates the "piggy back concept on the Utica Division.. Photo by Ronald Furner.

THE CABOOSE

The Caboose is the strange looking red or other brightly colored car at the end of the freight train used for shelter for the trainmen. For a long time, red was the common color and later the caboose took on the color of the railroad line.[49] A caboose was also on the end of the work train that delivered materials or carried away scrap. Oh, how I loved to ride in the caboose, especially resting on those bed-like flat cushions in the upper part of the caboose adjacent to the windows. The word caboose is derived from French and English words and used in reference to railroading since 1859.[50]

---

[49] John Wickre, American Steam, p. 79.
[50] B.A. Botkin and A.F. Harlow(Ed.), A Treasury of Railroad Folklore., p. 346.

RAILROAD DAYS

The long freight train or "rattler" rumbled down the track- sometimes at a slow speed and other times it traveled very fast.

The trainmen, the conductor, and the brakemen rode in the caboose. The conductor, as mentioned in an earlier chapter, is in charge of the train, and the caboose served as his office. Located at the top of the caboose is a cupola with padded bunks

George Perrone of Utica, NY, a former trainman, referred to the caboose as a "home" on the rails pointing out that sometimes in Binghamton, the crew would stay in the caboose overnight before returning to Utica. "Usually, if I went down on the "Bull," to Binghamton, the crew went over to the railroad YMCA to get a meal and then go to bed." Of course, the work train also had a caboose and I used to like to climb up there and lie down when we traveled from one work site to another. A pot bellied stove was kept loaded with coal to provide heat. It was always exciting to ride in the caboose with the trainmen.

The caboose as a part of the freight train was phased out in the 1980's since there are fewer trainmen on trains, and because computers have reduced much of the paperwork formerly done by the conductor.[51]

---

[51] Douglas Preston, President of Utica and Mohawk Valley Chapter of the National Railroad Historical Society. –August 12, 2005.

PEOPLE OF THE RAILROAD

THE TRAINMEN

Working summers, I had an opportunity, at times, to ride in the cab of the steam engine once in a while. I did get to know some of the trainmen. For example, engineers Henry "Hank" Williams, Frank Haines, and "Fritz" Cronauer, G.W. Penner, conductor, Earl Tinker, flagman, and Lester Conklin, conductor. My father had talked of others, for example, Jimmy Mack, engineer, and conductor, John Coughlin. He also said that Coughlin had died of undulant fever after drinking raw milk I learned additional information about the unfortunate incident from John Coughlin's son.

...On July 4, 1942, my Dad, John Coughlin, Sr. was working the milk train, switching cars around at the Bordens Milk Station in Norwich. My father and other train crewmen often obtained free milk from the milk station. He drank some of the milk and by the time he got home that day he became very sick and came down with a high fever. It was July 4, his birthday. He died twenty-three days later.[52]

When I interviewed my father, he told me that the train crew consisted of an engineer,[53] fireman, conductor, and three brakemen for trains over 25 cars. If under 25 cars, there would be

---
[52]John Thomas Coughlin Interview, June 7, 2005.
[53]Ibid.

fewer trainmen. Ed Luther of Poland, NY who worked as a trainman with the New York Central and the DL&W RR, verified this information about train crewmen. He also added that the three flagmen or brakemen were known as the 'head-end man" who rode in the cab of the engine, a "middle man" who rode either in the cab of the engine or in the caboose, and the "end man" who rode in the caboose. Luther had worked for the New York Central before his employment with the DL&W and Erie-Lackawanna and then with Conrail.

John Swald of Oriskany Falls, a former brakeman and conductor, worked for the Erie-Lackawanna. In the 1960's, he said that trains required five trainmen regardless of the length of the train.

Originally there was disagreement amongst the engineer, the conductor and the railroad hierarchy as to who was in charge of the train. It was decided that the conductor, a former brakeman or flagman, was actually in command of the whole train. The brakeman and flagman had dual duties, working the brakes on individual cars, controlling runaway cars, and duties giving signals with the red flag or red lantern as an emergency sign to stop a train.

George Perrone, a retired conductor, originally worked as a trackman for his father, John, whose section included the Utica Yard. George worked for seven years in the Maintenance of Way

Department until 1942 when he became a Utica Yard brakeman and later a conductor.

"The work of a brakeman or flagman is dangerous because of the possibility of falling off a freight car and being run over by a train. The railroad cars are equipped with a safer type coupling replacing the link and pin coupling for connecting cars. Link and pin coupling sometimes led to the loss of fingers or other injuries," Perrone related. The late Howard Berg of Clinton, in an interview with Douglas Preston of New Hartford, in 1996, relates the hazards of being a brakeman in an account of an accident that occurred to his father." Dad had been severely injured at Brisbane when he was a brakeman when the engineer jerked the train severely. Dad went down between the cars and lost both of his legs and for the rest of his life he had to walk on two artificial legs.[54]

---

[54] Douglas Preston, The Lackawanna in West Utica, An Interview with Howard and Harry Berg.(Pamphlet), Occasional Paper 18, Oneida County Historical Society. 1996.(Originally written for Tower Topics, Utica and Mohawk Valley Chapter of the National Railway Historical Society. September and November 1979.

Track behind station at Richfield Junction. 1942 rock slide. Section Foreman, Fred Julian, and Henry Cittadino with pickaxe, Joe Beretta(goggles), Ben Julian, (Hands on rock). Back-L-R: Sam Beretta, Tony Damiano, and George Nicotera. Photograph by Ed Bryant. Collection of Theodore Jackson.

Rock slide at Richfield Junction sidetrack behind the station. Left-Lester Bryant, Right-Section Foreman, Fred Julian. Wedged plow on tracks and section hand bending over operating a screw spike wrench. Photograph by Ed Bryant. Collection of Theodore Jackson

RAILROAD DAYS 45

Maintenance of Way Department – Small gang at work in west Utica adjacent to Utica arterial. Section foreman Louis Langone Sr. holding grandson, Robert Langone.-1962.

Erie-Lackawanna high railer was used to travel on highway and railroad. Note the small flanged wheels that are raised and lowered as needed. Section foreman Louis Langone, Sr. and grandson, Robert Langone. 1962. Photograph by author.

THE SECTION FOREMAN

A section foreman has many privileges that help make his work pleasant, but if a fellow is inclined to abuse these privileges, then he becomes soft, he loses his desire to do his best....I could name a lot of foreman that I have been associated with in my forty years of service that thought they could beat the game by doing only what was necessary to get by.....[55]

Rocco Langone, my grandfather, was the first in my family to work as a section foreman. Barely five feet tall and of slight build, Grandpa left Italy in 1888 for South America, perhaps seeking employment. In his travels to the New World, he visited Montevideo, Buenos Aires, and also the island of Cuba. After four years of traveling to the West, he returned to Italy in 1892 to bring his family with him and immigrate to the United States. Once here, they settled in Cassville, NY that same year.

Like so many of the immigrants, he looked to the railroad for employment. He was hired as a section man on the Utica Division the DL&W . The job required using tools such as long tamping bars (sometimes referred to as "widow makers")[56] to force cinder ballast under the crossties. The work also involved

---

[55] D.E. Gelwix, <u>Letters From An Old Section Foreman to His Son</u>, (Letter No.4, Omaha, NE, Railway Educational Bureau, p. 13, 1935.(Copyright D.C. Buell.
[56] Perrone, op.cit.

pumping the hand cars that were so common in the years before the motorized track car.

Grandpa worked long hard days in 1892 for $.10 an hour, ten hours a day, six days week (about $25.00 a month.) Advancing to section foreman by 1906, he earned about $35-$40 a month. As foreman, he managed sections in Cassville and Richfield Springs and each at that time was about two miles long.[57] He retired from the railroad in 1937. He worked hard, and in his spare time enjoyed cultivating a big garden, playing cards and the accordion, and loved to drink beer or wine with his Polish friends at the neighborhood Clayville bar. Blessed with much common sense, one of his favorite Italian accented phrases when he tended to disagree was –"That's a-not- a-practical."

His son, Louis, Sr., my father, was born in Cassville in 1902. Rocco Langone and his family moved to Richfield Springs, NY in 1907, the year after making section foreman and returned to Cassville in 1910 or 1911.

I have often thought of my father as one of the last of the company men. Though not perfect, he seemed to be always devoted to his work, the railroad was his life. Always taking pride in his work, he supervised the section workers under him fairly and compassionately.

---

[57] Ibid.

At the age of 14, Louis (my father) worked summers as a crossing watchman at North Bridgewater, NY. Grandpa took the section at Cassville and Louis attended school in Sauquoit. He quit school and went to work full time on the railroad earning $1.40 or $1.60 a day in 1916.

...There were no unions. They had started but didn't "pan out." They re-started in 1918, but even then no one belonged except crossing watchmen. The foremen belonged to a non-union supervisory organization that didn't amount to very much until about 1935 during President Franklin Roosevelt's administration.[58] The supervisory organization got "knocked out" so they (trackmen and foremen) all belonged to the same union. I remember that in the early days of the Union, one guy ran off with the dues. He got quite a bundle."

...I remember when World War I ended in 1918, we were working on Schuyler Street. The whistle sounded and one hundred men who were working there, walked off the job and got drunk. The tools were picked up and the job was closed.[59]

My father was a relief foreman for two to three years until 1924, the year he took over the section in Hubbardsville where the author was born in 1931. The section foreman was a salaried employee and not paid for overtime. He was paid about $179 a month and since the Depression began in 1929, the section in Hubbardsville was eliminated. And he took the section at Richfield Junction at Cassville in 1930. He drove back and forth and also rode the train until the family moved to Clayville in 1932 where

---

[58] Louis C. Langone, Sr. Audiocassette-1977.
[59] Louis C. Langone, Sr. interview – 1977,

we lived for six years. There were bad memories of the Great Depression.

My father related bad memories for many railroad workers during the Depression.

> ...The first thing they did was cut the help and the sections were lengthened. They made the work tougher for those that did work. There was no pay on rainy days. They cut that out too. If it rained in the morning, the help was held for three hours and then released. Laborers were released but foreman were held on the job. I got pneumonia when the depression started in 1929 and I was off for two months -but was paid. I had leg trouble in Clayville between1935-1937 and I wasn't paid all of the while. I was paid two or three weeks or a month then lost time. I went on the crossing as a watchman in Clayville in 1938 before obtaining a section in Earlville.[60]

In 1938, "Pa took the section in Earlville for two years and then the section in North Brookfield in 1940. Generally, railroads are divided into several divisions and each one of those, such as the Utica Division, is sub-divided into sections. Sections changed length in size over the years but "Pop's" section sixty-nine was nine miles long. While headquartered in North Brookfield, his section extended from Poolville Pond to the north of Waterville, to a milepost beyond the former Haxton Foods Co., now known as the Louis J. Gale and Son Feed and Fertilizer Co.

Assigned four to six men, "Pa" supervised the maintenance of the track in all seasons. He supervised work trains and snow

---

[60] Ibid.

removal operations. Snowstorms often required the use of plows and/or Jordan Spreaders[61] attached to locomotives so that the trains could pass through. Crossings and switches also had to be kept clear of ice build-up.

The author often helped with the time sheets and time books, which had to be sent in daily to the foreman's supervisor, the roadmaster in Syracuse.

My father and grandfather supervised sections of track at various places along the Utica Division sections. Rocco Tofalo of West Winfield (whose wife was a distant relative of my mother, supervised part of the Richfield Springs branch. The author's uncle, Fred Julian, also was a section foreman on the Richfield branch and after John Perrone retired, the Utica Yard was added to my Uncle Fred Julian's section. Working in the Utica Yard was unique and different from the single track and the fewer passing sidings in the sections of the outlying areas. Many companies in Utica, New Hartford, Yorkville and Whitesboro communities did business with the DL&W, and the section included many sidetracks with numerous switches.

Our family moved to Waterville in 1940 with the railroad section headquarters at North Brookfield. The tool house was located on the west side of the tracks across from the former Kling feed mill and coal yard.

---

[61] Jordan Spreader- Attached ahead of a work train locomotive to plow snow in the winter or perform right-of-way work in other seasons of the year.

RAILROAD DAYS

The ride to North Brookfield each morning in the 1941 Ford was a short six mile trip and Joe Banville and Bill Hickey, both residents of Sangerfield, rode along with us. I recall the World War II gas ration stamp, a large letter A, I think, in the right corner of the windshield. Parking the car along a side track leading to Kling's Mill, we walked across the tracks to the tool house. "Don't step on the rail. Step over it so you don't trip," "Pop" would say. He would then get the daily train lineup from the station agent who acquired it from the dispatcher in Utica or Binghamton. The schedule of trains and their location during the day was essential before the track car was placed on the rails to commence the work routine for the day.

  At the worksite, the track car would be removed at either a grade or farm crossing. At certain intervals there were take-off ramps made from cinders and two railroad ties. If a sidetrack was available, the track car would be left there for the day. Very often it was necessary to obtain up to date train locations so that the track would be safe for traffic. Also, the track car would not be put back on the track until this information was gathered. A portable phone with long poles with metal attachments at the top was carried on the track car. Western Union wire on utility poles existed on the right of way and one of us would hold the pole. The pole had two hooks with a spring attached to extend the hook up or down. A section hand would handle the pole and reach up and connect to the two wires closest to the tracks. (Western Union wires). Applying a downward pressure to the wires, phone contact was made with the train dispatcher in Utica or Binghamton and the section foreman would communicate on the portable phone. The phone did work most of the time. Passenger trains traveled on timetable schedules but there were many times, however, when we could not count on schedules. Also, it was difficult for freight trains to follow an exact timetable schedule. On one occasion near the GLF(Grange League Federation) in Hubbardsville, we were raising track and tamping ties on a hot July day. Because of the extreme heat, the track had buckled in the form of a large S. A whistle of a freight train was heard in the distance and the train had to be stopped. "Grab a flag and two torpedoes," my father shouted. I ran to the track car, grabbed a red flag and two small torpedoes (small explosives with a flexible lead strap to place on the ball of the rail at two different locations. (For a long time the torpedo was considered the smallest and most essential item used in railroading. "Nothing quite so reliable that gives a flagman such sense of security as the good old properly placed track torpedo.")[62] I raced up the track in a northerly direction and on the engineer's side of the track (right side of the cab). I wanted to make sure the engineer could see me and I saw the train approaching in the distance. I had to run far enough to allow sufficient room for the train to stop. After attaching the torpedoes to the ball of the rail, I

---

[62] Botkin, B.A. and Harlow, Edwin F.(Ed.), pp.343,347, A Treasury of Railroad Folklore.

then raced in the opposite direction, positioning myself on the side of the tracks and started waving the red flag so that the engineer could see it. I succeeded in stopping the train and saw "Hank" Williams of Cassville, the engineer, with his railroad hat and red bandana around his neck. Hank was a friendly old-timer, but he found it necessary to educate me so he proceeded to give me a lecture on how to flag a train. Climbing down from his cab, Hank took the flag. "You have to stand in the middle of the tracks and wave the red flag from one side to the other," Hank instructed me with firmness in his voice as he moved the flag in that manner. I reported back to my father and told him what Hank had said. "Hank is a safety man and he was just explaining the proper or recommended way to flag a train," my father explained. I always remembered that but I never had to flag another train.

Hank and his wife "Chrissie" lived for many years in Cassville not far from the tracks and it was said that he used to toot the whistle for "Chrissie" when he passed by with his train. I recall the front of his house was inscribed with large letters – Henry and Chrissie. He was one of the more colorful engineers. Ed Luther, a retired trainman, said that on Hank Williams' last day, he was engineer in the Utica Yard and an unfortunate incident occurred.

...It was a Sunday and we were in a hurry and an unfortunate incident occurred A brakeman had unlocked the derail and while we were up at the Sitroux plant a kid had thrown the derail. Hank brought the train down and went over the derail and the engine went off the track. However, no one was hurt.

The roadmaster was the supervisor of all section foremen on the Syracuse Division, the Utica Division and Richfield Springs Branch. The headquarters of the roadmaster was Syracuse and the roadmaster I knew was Clifford Graham. His son Randall also worked on the railroad and became a section foreman and roadmaster. One of the first big words (*copacetic*) I added to my vocabulary was one I learned from the roadmaster. One day at quitting time, after everything and everyone was loaded on the track cars and push cars, I remember him saying. "Is everything copacetic?" With that question – we were ready to go back to the tool house in North Brookfield. I had never heard that word before and decided from that day forward that I would add a new word to my vocabulary

The section foreman and roadmaster sometimes disagreed with the manner of doing the work but there generally were good relations with friendly lunch hour poker games and after work sessions at the Ye Olde American Hotel in Waterville – a local watering hole.

Crossing watchmen were also under the supervision of the section foreman. In Waterville, on the corner of White Street adjacent to the Bowling Alley driveway entrance, stood a shack for the watchman. Supplementing the bells and lights at the crossing, the watchman also held a stop sign whenever trains approached.

William Doyle, who worked part time with me shoveling snow in the winter, pointed out that there used to be a tower mounted atop the watchman's shack. "Jay Snow, Frank Wrobel and Phil Yapaolo were crossing watchmen," Doyle recalled. Lynn Williams of Waterville indicated that Michael McGlinn preceded Jay Snow on the crossing. After the watchman's position was eliminated, they worked as section men in the gang and the author recalls Wrobel and Yapaolo working as flagmen for the large "extra gangs" during track raising projects. Today, the only remnant to the watchman's shack is a concrete foundation with a small tree growing from it. In the extra gang when the major track raisings took place, they were assigned as flagmen at either end of the work site to flag trains to either lower their speed or to come to a complete stop.

After Fred Julian retired, my father was section foreman for a few years in the Utica Yard and south of Utica to Richfield Junction, and the Richfield Branch. The section also included the old O&W RR tracks to the former Carparelli business and Mohawk Container in New Hartford. The Blue Line, from Schuyler Street to Yorkville was also part of the section. The businesses Foster Paper and Dunlop were serviced by the railroad.

Louis Langone Sr. retired from the Erie-Lackawanna in 1967 after 53 years on the railroad and my eldest brother, Rocco, then followed as a section foreman. Rocco had started on the railroad in 1941 before entering the Army in 1942. When he came back from the war, he worked in the gang as a section hand and Assistant and/or Relief Foreman.

In the late 1960's, having the summer off as a teacher, and needing a job, Rocco hired me. Each morning I rode into Utica with him and Bob Masca to the Utica Yard section gang headquarters. In the Utica Yard I became familiar with the roundhouse and shops where the machinists worked. The old Erie-Lackawanna freight house is still located below the former location of the section gang tool house. I noticed that summer that the old yellow motor (track) car was long gone, replaced by the high railer as our mode of transportation on the tracks at that time. This vehicle, which my father also used before retirement, was operated on both the rails and highway.

My brother-in-law, Winfred Michel "Mike", started on the railroad in 1947. Before being assigned as a section foreman on the Syracuse Division, he was a car knocker and section hand. Car knockers work in the Yard and repair journal boxes, wheels and brakes of railroad cars. Cars needing major repairs were placed on the "cripple track." This was located near the old roundhouse in the Utica Yard. Mike also described how broken rails sometimes required cutting the replacement rail, which was sometimes longer than the broken rail to be removed. Acetylene torches were seldom available so a cold chisel would be used to mark the rail. One man held the chisel while another used the sledge to strike it repeatedly to leave an indentation along a cross-section of the rail.

Then several men lifted the rail first the waist and then as high as possible. On a command by the section foreman, the rail would be dropped and simultaneously the men would step back fast from the descending rail. A perfect break resulted and the rail would then be placed exactly in the track

Mike recalled the following about track work:

...Lifting a hundred pounds was nothing for a section man.. The jacks used for raising joints weighed seventy-one pounds. The aluminum jacks were lighter. Rail benders were used on the stock rail of a switch. As the stock rail was held in place, the rail bender would bend the steel rail to the proper angle. When we unloaded ties from the gondola cars on work trains, so many would be dropped off at the Western Union poles that had a numeral written on them on a previous day indicating the number to be thrown off along the right of way at that location. I remember a guy named Fenton who used to drive his tractor to work in Waterville. We could hear the tractor coming down the hill in the morning. Pop" had trouble seeing when he got his new bifocals. One time working on a bridge, he had trouble walking the ties since the ties are spaced fairly close together. He said that he was going to throw those bifocals away and get reading glasses.

Catherine Corleto Langone. Representative of the multitude of railroad wives who gallantly supported their husbands and children who worked as railroaders.

THE RAILROAD WIFE

A good many years ago when I would start out in the middle of the night during a bad storm to see if everything was right and the line was open, your mother would try to tell me that my trip was unnecessary....but I went just the same, Son....Now when I climb out of bed....she helps me with my boots.....she has learned that duty means more than personal comfort...[63]

Often taken for granted by men, women have not always been given the credit they really deserve. Railroad wives, like farmer's wives, rose early in the morning to prepare breakfast and lunches, since railroad men left for work at a very early hour. In some families, where two or three members were employed on the railroad, three or even more lunches had to be prepared. In those days, few men ever prepared their own breakfast, or lunch.

Catherine Langone, the author's mother, was one of these railroad wives. She started her day bright and early to prepare breakfast and lunches for several railroad men in the family.

Bruce McLean, formerly from Waterville, recalled the big lunch his mother used to prepare when he worked in the section gang one summer. "Each day she made eight sandwiches for me to take to work," McLean noted.

Gerald Furner recalled the good times the section men had after work at the local pubs, especially Ye Olde American Hotel in Waterville. Their wives often called there since on pay day, the men took a bit longer time to get home. Stopping by the pub first, the late Robert Masca related the following remembrance of working for the author's father: "There were times we would stop after work on Oriskany Street, the Oriskany Street Grill,

---

[63] D.E. Gelwix, Letters From An Old Section Foreman to His Son, Omaha, NE, Railway educational Bureau, p. 31, 1935.(Copyright D.C. Buell

sometimes referred to as the "Hole in the Wall", to unwind. Back then the draft beers were only ten cents.. Some of the wives were not too happy." Railroad work could create quite a thirst after a long day in the sun and my mother waited many a night for the railroad men to come home.

When "Pop" had the section in Hubbardsville in the late 1920's, the roadmaster visited at the house. We always had a barrel or two of hard cider and my father had asked my mother to bring out the jug of cider. Mother brought it out and my father had recalled that the roadmaster, Mr. Schofield, took a drink of cider and after making an awful face, had remarked. "My God, this tastes like vinegar." The vinegar jug had been in the same area and we were never sure if this were a mistake or intentional to persuade the roadmaster to leave. We think it was a mistake but we had always enjoyed a big laugh when "Pop" told the story.

Sometimes, a derailment, track wash-out, or winter weather in general called for overtime work and late hours thus leaving wives and children alone at home. Linda Nichols, my niece, remembers how sometimes her father, Rocco did not come home for two or three nights during the winter. "Dad would send his check home by train to Mom so she could buy groceries."

Despite all this the women of the railroad families learned to accept these ways. And over the years the wives and mothers heard a large amount of "railroad talk." Terms such as "switch," (Mother pronounced it the "sweetch.", "wash-out," "frog," "the

Branch," "the local," were added to their vocabulary. The numbers assigned to the passenger and freight trains, and station stops, became as familiar to many of the wives as the daily soap operas my mother enjoyed.

NYS&W RR crosstie machine inserting ties into the tracks during the summer of 2003. Usually two to four men used tie tongs to remove and insert ties on the Utica Division in the 1940's

Rail Lifter lifts rails as two NYS&W Railway Co. trackmen position tie plates between rail and crosstie during the summer of 2003. Plates placed manually on the Utica Division in the 1940's.

THE TRACKMAN (GANDY DANCER)

GANDY DANCING – PAST AND PRESENT

"And it's joint ahead and center back, and Jerry go and ile (sic)that can." Carl Sandburg's American Songbook[64]

In railroad jargon a Gandy Dancer is a section hand or trackman. This slang expression dates to the 19th century, and there was a song later, in the 1940's, entitled the "Gandy Dancer's Ball." I was hired in the summer of 1944 and the world was still at war. Even though I was only thirteen, my father hired me on the railroad. Paul Brocker wanted to hire me for his father's farm off Route 20 in the town of Sangerfield. "Pop" was afraid I was going to get hurt on the farm. He happened to mention the farm job offer to the assistant roadmaster, his immediate supervisor. He said, "Let's hire him on the railroad." It was wartime and there was a manpower shortage. The supervisors bent the rules and I became a section hand. The minimum wage in 1940 was $.36 an hour and in 1944 I was paid $.65 an hour, which I contributed to the family income. On my first day of work I met Bill Messenger, a signal maintainer from Norwich. He said, "So you want to be a "Gandy Dancer," and another new term was added to my vocabulary. As

---

[64] Richard Reinhardt, <u>Workin' On the Railroad</u>, Palo Alto, American West Publishing Co, 1970.

noted above, the term "Gandy Dancer" originated during the 19th century and probably got its name from the manufacturer of a short handled shovel with a narrow width called a Banjo and used by track laborers. I immediately learned that the Banjo used on the tracks was not a stringed musical instrument but a unique short handled shovel used for tamping cinder ballast under ties. It was the only banjo I ever learned to "play" and working with that shovel to tamp cinders under ties was one of the most boring jobs I have ever had to endure. Referring to a regular member of the gang, George Pierson, a North Brookfield farmer and part-time member of the section gang, remembered tamping with the banjos. He mentioned Charles Nolan, who lived in the Sangerfield area, and was a regular in the section gang. "He worked for your Dad, you know. Charlie and I were partners when we tamped ties." Tamping involved the placing of ballast, (cinders on the Utica Division), under the ties. Usually, the workers tamped opposite one another next to the rail with "banjo" shovels. "I didn't dare use Charlie's shovel," Pierson said. "All of the regular section men such as Charlie had their own "banjo" shovel. You didn't dare to use theirs or they would get mad. They would actually mark their shovel to identify it."

  The section gang maintained highway grade crossings and made them passable for automobiles. Often the gang had to spread asphalt or "blacktop." We called it "hot mix" as opposed to coalprovia ("cold mix" The men worked fast to apply it to the crossing before the mixture hardened. Small bon-fires were started to heat the banjo shovels so that the asphalt could be spread more easily. During that first summer in 1944 a large truck of asphalt was delivered to Earlville for a crossing in the vicinity. I believe it was one of Laino's trucks from Utica. My father assigned me to ride with the driver to direct him to the correct crossing. The rest of the gang would go by track car to meet the truck. I had an approximate idea of where the crossing was and so we took off up and down a couple of hills and some right hand turns in the direction of the crossing. Needless to say I was somewhat apprehensive. Along the way, somewhat gruff and skeptical of this very young teen-ager, questioned me along the way with a doubt in his voice as to whether we would get to the right crossing. Fortunately (and with great relief), I remembered the route. I have often thought of what it would have been like if I had directed that big truck with all of that "hot mix" to the wrong crossing. How long would it have taken to get to the right crossing? Remember, back then cell phones did not exist to call ahead for directions or to explain possible delays.

Recently, while observing a current NYS&W RR tie replacement project, my thoughts drifted back to 1946 and 1947 when hundreds of railroad crossties were being replaced by trackmen of the old DL&W RR... In the 1940's, a special extra gang of thirty-five men plus small gangs from other sections of the division replaced crossties and raised the track along the 86-mile railroad branch that includes the Nine-Mile Swamp and Waterville.

In 2003 the NYS&W was engaged in an extensive project replacing crossties in the roadbed along the Utica Division where 50,000 of them were inserted. Observing the operation, I saw the machines move down the tracks replacing ties for the NYS&W and I could smell that familiar odor of the freshly creosote -dipped ties. I recalled those days of long ago when I worked for my Dad. I remembered when these old, battered, and now replaced crossties were brand new sometime around 1947.

The yellow colored machines of the NYS&W RR moved steadily down the rails with steady precision accomplishing what the workers of the 1940's did then mainly by hand. I remembered when we had used heavy steel tie tongs, short handled shovels, seventy-one-pound cast iron jacks, claw bars, and lining bars. Small gangs of five or six men used this simple equipment to replace ties when needed.

In the 1940's a major project took place along the Utica Division that included the laying of heavier rail and then raising the track several inches, replacing about 50-75 ties per day. (Some of the old ties were of the pre-World War I era). New ties used to be unloaded by hand from "gons" (gondola freight cars). If you forgot, or did not have gloves, your hands would be covered with black creosote. Sometimes, the creosote caused blisters on the forearms or a finger would be banged between the tie and the steel side of the gondola. Bill Hickey who worked as a high school student also remembered the blisters on the arms that the creosote caused from handling the ties.

Trackmen would remove the spikes and tie plates from the old ties and then the old ties would be pulled out using large tie tongs. Most of the time there were two to four men required for the more stubborn removals. After extracting the old ties, they were left along the railroad right of way or sometimes pushed down the bank. Later they would be piled and burned. The old ties still had some odor of creosote, and sometimes complaints came from homeowners along the tracks because of the smoke and odor from the burning ties. Truckloads of old ties were given away to farmers and to others who wanted old ties for various uses, such as fence posts. New ties were positioned in the track about 21 inches apart and after placing the tie plates by hand, cinder ballast was then tamped under the ties with the banjo shovels bringing the ties up to the tie plates that were placed by hand. Cut spikes place in two of the tie plate holes and then hammered manually into the ties

As my reflections returned to the present, I continued to gaze with wonder at the procession of machines and the ease in which the NYS&W RR employees removed and replaced the ties with this newer technology that has been in use for several years. .I could almost hear the grunts and the groans from the past of two to four men, on the tie tongs pulling to release a huge oversized tie from the road bed. Now, I noticed that if the opening in the track bed was not quite large enough for the tie-extracting machine, the new tie was eased back and forth by the clawed arm. Other machines waited patiently to perform their function. A tamping machine followed pushing crushed stone under the ties. The ballast regulator with a sweeper mounted swept the ties clean of excess crushed stone or old cinder ballast.

In the old days, ashes or cinders obtained from coal burned on the steam engines, was used as ballast. Crushed stone has since replaced cinders as ballast. Hopper freight cars that were loaded with cinders were shipped in from points south. Unloading cinders proved the dirtiest of all of the jobs.

As the modern operation continued, a rail lifter machine that was being operated by a man on both sides of the track, lifted the rail just enough to position the tie plates (that had been spread by hand), into place. The men used a tool to shove the plate in place and then lower the rail. A spiking machine that drove cut spikes through the opening in the plate and into the tie followed behind. A tamping machine then forced ballast under the ties.

RAILROAD DAYS 69

NYS&W Railway Co. spiking crossties with spiking machine during summer of 20003machine. Spiking ties manually with a spiking hammer was a strenuous task for the section hand (trackman.). Not striking the spike squarely could lead to flying spikes and cause serious injury.

Some machines, such as spike pullers, were used back in the 1940's. I occasionally used a screw wrench that removed screw spikes (preceded cut spikes) from the ties. On the larger jobs, air compressors were used for air hammers that drove spikes into ties. Most of the time trackmen spent whole days spiking with strange looking narrow shaped spiking hammers. Sometimes we would miss a spike and hit the rail and the shock was painful. Spiking was a job that I tried to avoid. Small steel nails (date nails) with the last two digits of the year imprinted on them, were pounded into the center of the new ties to mark the year when there were inserted into the roadbed. The railroad did not use date nails after 1947, probably to cut cost.

When asked as to how many men were needed for the project to replace ties, one of the NYS&W RR foremen told me that their tie gang consisted of 21 men who can replace 1000 to 1200 ties a day. I also learned that some of the employees are paid $12 to $18 an hour and worked a four-day week. The foreman smiled with surprise when I told him that I was paid $.65 an hour when I first started on the railroad in 1944 and worked eight hours, six days a week.

Following the replacement of ties, spiking and tamping of ballast, the last step I observed was the unique lining machine that followed bizarre looking lining equipment on the tracks. The removal and replacement of ties made it necessary to realign the tracks. When I worked on the railroad six men and six lining bars were used to line track. There would be three men on each side of the track and inside the track. They would insert the point of the bar under the rail between the ties. The section foreman, standing at a distance would line the track by eye giving these commands. Joint ahead!. Center back! Quarter back! Give it hell! "Just a little! One man with the bar would reply – 'Yo!. And the track would move sometimes too far and the foreman would yell with disapproval.

RAILROAD DAYS

Donald Chirlin of Norwich, NY a friend and fellow teacher at West Winfield, once worked for two summers on the New York Ontario and Western Railroad. He told me a story very similar to the above account of lining track with the lining bars. He said the foreman would look down the track and would give a command similar to the above,. "Joint ahead, or "Just a little". One man in the gang would yell "Yo," Chirlin recalled. And the privilege to be the one who would say "Yo" was guarded selfishly. The work of the section man does not differ much from one railroad to another.

Modern technology, introduced in the last forty years has generally replaced the use of several men with lining bars. In observing the NYS&W unique lining machinery working in the Waterville area, I saw only one man operating the machine. Equipment ahead of the machine on the rails had a red sensor light that gave information to the operator on a computer screen how much to move the track. On that day the machine was working on a curve (1-2°).

Many years ago I had helped a curve liner from Syracuse named Ace. Stakes were placed around a curve and strings were held from the rail to the stakes and Ace would record measurements around the curve. He then calculated measurements for my father when the time came to line that particular curve. At times, I recall my father disagreeing with the figures and once discarded them relying more on his eye. Gerrit Hyde backed this up by remembering one time when he was one of the men with a lining bar helping to line a curve after some ties were replaced and the track was raised near the feed mill in Waterville. "Ace," the curve liner or engineer had given my father some mathematical calculations. Hyde said that after "Ace" left, my father threw the figures away and lying down on his stomach and looking through a small red block of wood with a small hole in it, he would give the commands on how far to move the track as it was being lined. "The result was a nice even curve," Hyde recalled.

Louis M. Langone, my nephew, worked for his dad, Rocco, during the summer of 1971 and also with the extra gang in 1974 at Scheidelman's in Utica next to the Route 12 arterial. The project was moving the tracks for the new bridge and he said that there were twelve men in the gang. Louis M. also recalled that during that same year a car on the siding was always going off the track when it was moved through the switch by the yard office. The problem was in the switch but difficult to correct. My father who was retired for seven years, was asked to come in to see if it could be fixed. Speaking admiringly of his grandfather, my nephew said that "Gramp" got down and eyed out the situation and found the problem. There were no derailments after that."

Leaving the worksite that day, I realized that the age of the spiking hammer and the long handled tie-tongs, and the lining bars are tools of a distant past. I thought once again of how muscle and brawn had built our nation's railroads. The days of the Gandy

RAILROAD DAYS

Dancer and his "daily dance" with the Banjo shovel, and the long lonesome whistle of the steam locomotive have become some of the happy memories of my youth.

The section gang was usually made up of six men and there were several sections of a few miles each on the division. At North Brookfield there used to be a tool house, a water tower for the steam engines, and a well that provided drinking water for thirsty section men and others in the area. At the time, we thought it was the coldest and best drinking water in the whole country.

My railroad experience included many jobs including water boy. My "Pop" did not want me to work too hard. My first job during a rail laying project was to place tie plates on the ties and spread spikes —one inside the rail and one outside the rail next to the tie plate. A crane operator named Duffy worked a crane type machine that had its own power and operated on the track with its own brakeman. He would pick up rails with this machine we called a Kohring (manufacturer's name). Trackmen attached the cable to the ball of the rail and the Kohring crane swung the rail over and down on to the tie plates. Robert Masca told me that one time in Clayville the Kohring crane lost power and started down the track uncontrolled. It was all down hill and Duffy was quite upset as it headed toward Higby Road. As it reached the flat it stopped near Higby Road. George Brill, the head mechanic, and Duffy were very stressed out, but fortunately it stopped without accident.

Ernest Clemens used to live next to the tool house in North Brookfield and worked during World War II while some regular workers went off to war. "Ernie" said he had a heart problem that disqualified him for the military.

…Because they could not get good men during the war years, they were willing to hire me as a section hand. Sometimes they had me as a section hand, and other times I was needed on the snow plow. I also got in some time firing and worked at other times as a flagman. Those were good days. I liked the railroad work. It was peaceful out in the back country away from automobiles and hub-bub. When winter was cold and blustery the station houses were a comfort. The Lackawanna was running three passenger cars a day both ways between Utica and Binghamton, plus many freighters.[65]

Section men were tough, rugged workers and experienced eight and more hours of strenuous labor every day – six days a week. "On September 1, 1949, the work week for maintenance of way employees was reduced through national agreement with the railroads from forty-eight to forty hours a week without reduction in weekly pay."[66]. As the teacher and his students sometimes looked forward to snow days, the section hand looked forward to an occasional rainy day with pay.

George Pierson and his brother Rodney, worked for my father in the early years of World War II. George recalled working with my oldest brother Rocco. Lee O'Brien, John Giedraitis,

---

[65] Ernest Clemens, ComeWalk With Me, .p. 93.
[66] Milestones of Progress, A Brief History of the Brotherhood of Maintenance of Way Employees (Pamphlet), p.9

Oscar Boutwell and Charles Nolan. George remembered that in 1942, he and my brother were cutting brush along the right of way with brush hooks. "I told 'Rocky'-'you be careful," George said. "This big prickly blackberry bush was 6-8 feet high. When you cut it off it will come back and hit you. 'Rocky' didn't listen." "Never mind," 'Rocky' replied. "Well, the bush swung back after he cut it and hit him in the face." 'Son-of-A-Bitch," Rocky said. "He didn't do that again," Pierson said.

Lee O'Brien worked in the gang for many years and was a big strong, pleasant man. "I worked with Lee O'Brien and we called him Bully, [67]Pierson stated. He was a comical old guy. One time we were cleaning snow from switches. I got mine all cleaned out because I was shoveling faster than 'Bully'. He got mad and would grab my shovel so I wouldn't beat him in cleaning the switch. He didn't want to be outdone. Pierson mentioned some of the same members of the gang.

Referring to another regular member of the gang, Pierson says,

I remember Oscar Boutwell of North Brookfield. I would kid with him and tell him to not let his girlfriend take all of his money. Boutwell served in World War II in Europe and the author remembers working with him a few summers after the War. He was a hard worker and hard drinker and I enjoyed working with him.

Pierson loved to joke around. Relating a joke he pulled on the boss, he described how they were working in Hubbardsville;

---

[67] The nickname was probably a reference to O'Brien having the strength of a bull or to "Bull" Montana, the professional wrestler and silent movie actor of the 1920's.

...We were working around a curve and couldn't see any trains that might be due. We were tightening bolts on the rail joints. We used a piece of hollow pipe attached to the wrench for leverage. As we were tightening bolts, I blew into the hollow end of the wrench extension and made a sound mimicking a train whistle. Oooooooo-oooooooo. Louie thought a train was coming and he pulled out his Hamilton railroad watch and remarked. 'It isn't time for the train yet.' Louie swore at me and we all had a big laugh.

With a loud laugh, Pierson also remembered another of his pranks.

That year we raised track from Sherburne to New Hartford. One time near the Waterville depot, we were raising track and your father would get down and sight the track for low joints or centers of the rail. He had slowed the train with a "slow order." I went to get a pail of water and I made a sign or whistle which caused the train to speed up. Your father yelled to slow that engineer down. He used to call me the "Puckerville Pirate" [68] Puckerville, neither hamlet nor village, is located a short distance from North Brookfield.

On another occasion, Pierson recalled that the boss brought some hot peppers to work and gave one to his brother, Rodney Pierson. "Boy, were they hot. Rodney's mouth burned so much he ran down the bank to .a nearby spring and plunged his head in the water. Everybody got a big laugh out of that."

The author remembers working with Lee O'Brien. He was very strong and he carried the huge cast iron jack and large lining

---

[68] Puckerville, neither village or hamlet, is located off Route 12 south of North Brookfield.

bar with great ease. I saw him put a very heavy rail bender (meant for bending a rail used in a switch) on his shoulder and carrying it several yards. Another time at lunch, he gave me a piece of meat from his lunch. I said to him, "This chicken is good." He replied it was woodchuck. The one and only time I ate woodchuck meat. He told me that you have to remove certain glands or nodes under the front legs of the woodchuck or it would give the meat a bad taste. Railroad work made me more worldly.

Ernest Clemens said he fondly remembered Lee O'Brien,. "He was a big man and they called him Bully. He sat in the front right spot on the track car and had a broom to sweep snow from the front of the car. No one dared take that seat." Clemens recalled working with Oscar Boutwell, John Giedraitis, and Joe Banville of Sangerfield. "Joe was a little guy and, unknown to the boss, he carried a little bottle with him and he often took a snort from it."

Clemens also remembered that John Giedraitis lived between North Brookfield and Brookfield and he owned a Graham Paige automobile but often walked several miles to the tool house in North Brookfield. Clemens recalled that one time the gang was laying rail between North Brookfield and Hubbardsville on a frosty morning. "The crane operator was having difficulty with the icy conditions," Clemens said. "I was handling rails as they swung into position off the car. A clutch slipped and a rail dropped on my foot, breaking it." Clemens continued to work with considerable pain. "Mr. Langone saw my problem and took me to Dr. Battles in Waterville. Kind man that he was, he knew I needed the money, so I was temporarily assigned as a crossing watchman to stop traffic at White Street in Waterville when trains approached," Clemens stated.

Clemens said he remembered when cutting rails was sometimes necessary to fit an opening when there was a broken rail. Since the rail was not of normal length and missing the pre-drilled holes, it was necessary to drill new holes at the end of the rail with a hand powered drill. It was then possible to insert the bolts to connect the angle bars placed at the rail joints.

Clemens described living near the tracks at North Brookfield and that he became used to the noise of the trains. He said that in those days, times were tough financially and the family would pick up soft coal dropped from the coal cars to burn in their stove, even though it "belched out black smoke from the chimney just like the steam engine. He was grateful to the firemen who would throw off huge blocks of that soft coal at the front of the house. Clemens recalled a little mischief he had become involved in while he was in school and long before he worked on the railroad. Taking some time off from school, he and a friend of his walked the tracks toward Paris from Waterville, counting the ties and placing objects to be crushed on the rails. This included stones, old railroad spikes and bolts. He said the next morning he was called in by the principal, Mr. Radley. Clemens said the section foreman and the gang happened to be traveling on the tracks that day and noticed the objects and reported the boys to the school. "I received some stings from a ping pong paddle. Clemens thinks that the section foreman was my father. The author's father pointed out that sometimes foreign objects were put on the tracks and these created a hazard for the trains. He told me of an incident on the main line of the DL&W RR when a spike placed in a small opening at one joint had caused a serious wreck. Before Bob Masca became foreman, he worked for my brother, Rocco, and he recalled that "Rocky" said we had to patrol the track with the high railer to Richfield Springs.

…We started out of Utica and made it to Bridgewater and Route 8. Just before we reached the crossing, the high railer went off the track and down an embankment. We were lucky that no one was hurt. We were later told that some kids playing on the track had placed a spike between the rails.

Several high school and college students worked during the summer months.. Bruce McLean, who grew up in Waterville worked on the railroad summers before he became a lawyer. He had worked for his uncle on the potato farm and was accustomed to hard work. However, he recalled how tough it was to work as a section hand and to spike ties and removing ties. "Pulling ties should have been done by horses rather than man."

…Every morning when I awoke my hands were locked in a tight fist. My mother had to insert a spoon between my fingers so I could eat my cereal in the morning. When I got to work we usually started with pulling ties and I could get my fingers around the tie tongs by 10 A.M. Then I could open my fingers enough to start spiking. It was the hardest physical work of my life. It made all the other physical work seem like a 'cup of tea.' I had worked on my uncle's farm but nothing could compare to the section gang. My mother packed eight sandwiches for me and I would eat two at ten o'clock, four at noon, and two in the afternoon. But we had a lot of fun with many jokes and all of the teasing from the conditioned regulars. It was the highest paying job at the time and this made college a lot more fun for the short time before I was called up for the service.[69]

McLean also remembered eating woodchuck that one of the men brought to work. "There was this thin guy who drank a lot and he always complained of his ulcer."[70]

During my first summer on the railroad, the boss assigned Bill Hickey and me to operate the bolt machine during the rail-laying project. After the angle bars were placed at the joints and bolts and nuts put into place, we followed with a bolt machine and sledge to tighten the bolts. The bolts have an oval thickening at the head that must be placed just right and then hit with a sledge before the tightening commenced. Sometimes it was difficult to get the bolt to stop turning. Hickey, who has traveled on the railroad in many parts of the world, has often noticed bolts missing from the rail joints. This had reminded him of how the both of us must have done a great job with the bolt machine. He also remembered that most of the work was done by hand including the

---

[69] Bruce McLean letter of December 14, 2003.
[70] Probably Oscar Boutwell who was a regular work in the author's father section gang.

handling of rail, working on the work trains on the top of Hopper cars, unloading cinders and the unloading of creosote covered ties that sometimes burned the skin. "The tracks are probably still polluted from the many tobacco chewers spitting along the tracks. I remember the poker games during the noon hour and sometimes I even operated the motor car (the track car)," he added.

Living in Sangerfield adjacent to the railroad, Hickey recalled the blizzards when trains got stuck in the snow. He felt lucky that he was permitted to get into the cab of the locomotive stuck in the snow, and shovel coal onto the fire.

NYS&W RR Tamping and Lining Machine. This machine tamped ballast under the ties and also lined (straightened) tracks electronically. Short narrow shovels were formerly used to tamp ballast under ties. The manual method of lining track was the use of six men with steel lining bars and the foreman lining the track by eye. Photograph by Adele Cooper.

THE "EXTRA GANG"

The summers of 1944-1948, when I worked on the section, and the summers of 1949 and 1950 were the years of the large gangs. During WWII one of the projects replaced the 80lb. rail on the Utica Division with 105lb. rail. The heavier rail was used from the main line (Hoboken to Buffalo) and used on the various divisions of the DL&W RR. Larger tie plates, larger cut spikes, different angle bars and larger bolts were required. Older type screw or smaller cut spikes had been used on the 80lb. rail. There were about 60 men in the extra gang compared to the average six man gangs of the individual sections. The section gangs joined the extra gangs each day and sometimes had to leave the extra gang for a job on the section. For example, to bury a cow struck by a train, repair a broken rail, or remedy some other situation on the foreman's own section.

The large extra gang was composed of temporary help. College students, high school students, part-time farmers, or others interested in working. Many of these college students later became teachers, lawyers, doctors, accountants, etc. Most of them were very good railroad workers. Elwyn Sterling, who later became a Colgate University language professor, remembers acquiring a huge blister on his hand. He then received a soft assignment of carrying water. In those days everyone drank out of the same water dipper. One of the jobs of the section men was using a scythe, (a difficult tool to use), to cut grass on the right of way. Sterling, from a farm family, was very good in using the scythe to cut grass.

The extra gang had a separate foreman and for most of the years that I worked, Clarence Simmons from Norwich was that foreman. Following the laying of rail, the raising of the track was necessary and Simmons supervised the gang for several summers. Since Simmons was the youngest foreman regarding seniority rights and did not have a section of track assigned to him, he had been appointed extra gang foreman. I always liked "Sim" and was treated right by him. Most of the time my father and "Sim" were able to get along and seldom disagreed except a time near Sangerfield. I do not remember the disagreement.

During World War II, probably because of the manpower shortage, age was sometimes overlooked. I was hired at age thirteen and the railroad had also hired Dick Simmons, Clarence's son, and also under age. Dick told this writer that his father worked for 40 years on the DL&W RR. "I worked for him two summers when I was sixteen on the summer extra gang. I laid rail from Greene to Oxford. I was supposed to be eighteen," Simmons said.

One summer the railroad hired real hoboes from out of the area and I remember that they lived in camp cars and they were big drinkers of alcohol.

RAILROAD DAYS

...We tried them out. They were good men but they didn't want to work. They'd work two or three days and then go out and get drunk. After one of these drunks, a couple of them were kidding around and one said to the other. How much money you got left? The other said about $.25 or $.50 left. The other hoboes would then kid him and call him a miser.[71]

Another summer Mexicans replaced the hoboes and they also lived in camp cars parked at the rail siding in Hubbardsville near the old GLF business.[72] Walter McKie, the station agent at Hubbardsville distributed the pay checks to the Mexicans and after receiving their checks would have to sign a form. McKie's, son, Albert, recalled his father telling him that some of the Mexican names were so long, it was impossible to get their whole name on the form.[73] The Mexicans often complained about their accommodations and on one occasion reported that the beans were infested with worms. The Assistant Foreman, Tommy, who communicated with them in Spanish, was asked by them to tell the extra gang foreman. The outfits that ran the camp cars did not seem to care very much and it seemed that no one really cared much.[74] The railroad provided the painters, welders and bridge gangs much better camp cars.

---

[71] Louis Langone Sr. Audiocassette, 1977
[72] Grange League Federation(GLF), a farm cooperative that was located in many communities, was later known for many years as Agway.
[73] Albert McKie, Interview, April 8, 2005.
[74] Ibid.

The author remembers when the Mexicans used to complain about their food and I used to like to sing with them. One of the songs I had heard from a cowboy movie was "Rancho Grande." I tried to get Sterling, who was taking Spanish in college to help me learn the words.

When the extra gang worked around Poolville, my father hired some Negro migrants. They lived in the building next to the tracks in Poolville. When I interviewed my father in 1977, he recalled, "What an outfit that was. The Mexicans and Negroes did not get along and the Mexicans had to have a separate pail of water. The Mexicans seemed to be more steady in their work. The Negroes wanted time off but they weren't bad workers." Once I remember working by the curve at Poolville Pond, a Black worker found a snapping turtle. He made the turtle grab a stick that he held and he then pulled its neck out. He then cut the neck off with his knife. I will always remember his comment to my father. "No points on that, Boss." He was referring to the meat rationing stamps required during World War II.

As the track raising and tie replacement operation approached Waterville in 1946 and 1947, my father took over the "extra gang." This operation involved the boring job of tamping cinders under ties with the banjo shovels.

A large horizontal raising board would be positioned several yards down the track. The tracks were about to be raised three to six inches. I would watch the extra gang foreman – either

RAILROAD DAYS

Clarence Simmons or my father, in the bib overalls, get down on all fours and look through a small red block of wood with a hole in the center. Another block of wood was held over a rail joint ahead and the foreman would line it up with the raising board in the distance. Trackmen on both sides of the tracks would insert a bar in a track jack that weighed over 70 pounds and raise the track as directed by the foreman. The foreman sighted through the peep hole to the top of the block held by the trackman and then sight to another spot on the raising board.[75] During the operation a level board with a bubble and adjustments checked the elevation for curves. A track gauge placed on the rails checked the width of the track, especially when putting spikes in the new ties. Proper gauge of four feet eight and one-half inches had to be maintained.

"Pop" had often mentioned the term "standard gauge" pointing out that it was the same all over the country. At the time it didn't seem like much to me. The gauge refers to the distance between the rails and standard gauge refers to the same width on all railroads-four feet and eight and one-half inches. Imagine what it must have been like when the gauge varied from one railroad to another. In 1871 there were 23 different railway gauges throughout the United States. The widest was six feet and the narrowest was three feet.[76] The track gauge mentioned above was

---

[75] Winfred Michel, Interview October 31, 2004.
[76] American Railroads, Their Growth and Development., Association of American Railroads, p. 23.

always carried on the track car. When replacing a rail or in raising the track, the section foreman always checked the gauge.

By 1868, the Utica, Chenango and Susquehanna Valley Railroad (later part of the DL&W RR), changed to standard gauge, moving each rail seven and three-fourths inches closer to the center and modifying the locomotives, was completed as far as Sherburne. The changeover on the Richfield Branch finished in 1872. By 1876, the DL&W RR changed completely to standard gauge.

Robert Fanning and Mary Susan(Fanning) Langone purchase tickets from ticket agent Guy Vining for a train ride from Waterville to Utica in 1947. Collection of Mary Susan (Fanning) Langone. Photograph by Dante Tranquille. Reproduced with permission of Utica Observer-Dispatch.

TICKET AGENT/FREIGHT AGENT

Of the station agents I met, three in particular stand out in my memory. All, Walter Collins, Jack Heenan, and Guy Vining lived in Waterville. Another agent, Grant Pughe, retired before I had the opportunity to meet him.

Since the Section 69 headquarters was at North Brookfield, I saw Jack Heenan almost every day at the station across from where the milk station used to be located. When we were working in or near the Swamp Road crossing, we either ate lunch at the tool house, inside the station and visited with Jack or sat near the siding by the driveway at Kling's where the men would park their cars. Sometimes at lunch, we would turn a car radio on and listen to a well known WSYR –Syracuse radio newscaster, relate the World War II news. Heenan also had to carry coal to keep the boiler going to make steam for the well pump to fill the huge water tank that supplied water for the locomotives. It was interesting to see the trainmen extend the long pipe out to the top of the locomotive and see the water gush into the huge steam engine. The old wooden tank by the side of the tracks is no longer there. Heenan replaced Walter Collins in Waterville after "Walt" became ill in the 1950's.

Guy Vining worked with Walter Collins as a telegrapher and ticket agent. Collins sold train tickets and also served as the freight agent responsible for completing the shipping and receiving paperwork. The passenger station in Waterville was located across from the old Waterville Textile Mill. Only a large flat slab of concrete remains there on the corner of Putnam Street and Conger Avenue.

The freight house stood diagonally across Putnam Street from the textile mill. In the late 19th century, Scranton Coal was located across from Putnam Hall (later location of Buell Boot and Shoe Manufacturers and Waterville Textile Mill).. Burt Regan operated this coal business in the 1940's. Various sidetracks

RAILROAD DAYS 91

serviced the businesses nearby. The first floor of Putnam Hall served for several years as the original passenger and freight station for the DL&W.

The Waterville Freight House. Formerly located across the street from the passenger station. Courtesy of Sherburne Historical Society.

I recall during World War II, when my father told Vining and Collins, who sent and received, Western Union telegrams, that if any telegrams from the War Department regarding my three brothers were received that he, and not my mother, was to be the first person notified. My father often had the section men help the station agents with some of their more physical duties such as carrying coal for stoves or boilers.

Pauline Collins Barnes, Walter's daughter, said that there were three shifts for station operators and that her father worked the second shift until Grant Pughe died. The shifts were reduced to two and Collins then worked days. Pauline Barnes recalled that her father belonged to the Order of Railroad Telegraphers' Union. She said that after her father received telegraphed train orders, he looped them into a wire on a stick. Then, the brakeman, standing on the step of the railroad car grasped the stick with the train orders from "Walt". Also, the railroad constructed structures with signal arms in front of some stations for train orders hoisted high enough for the engineer or fireman to grab them.

Barnes explained how she rode the passenger trains:

...I used to ride the train from Utica to Waterville when I attended the Utica School of Commerce in 1930. I would walk from Bank Place to Union Station to catch the train. Also, my mother and I often rode the train and we used the railroad pass given to spouses and family members of employees. One time my mother rode the train to Utica at 7:00 A.M. but did not arrive home until 11:00 P.M. The railroad made a schedule change and my father didn't tell my mother that the departure of the 5:30 P.M. leaving Utica had been changed. Once in Waterville the train waited for my mother and me. Rushing to get to the train my aunt went ahead and yelled to the conductor. "Stop", she hollered, "Walt Collins wife wants to get on.' The conductor (Youmans), had already said 'All aboard.' But he did delay the departure. My father also sold train tickets. Wearing his uniform cap (similar to a conductor's cap), he would move to the passenger train section of the station where was a separate area for the ladies. The ladies and men would form separate lines to purchase tickets. Children would like to take the train from Waterville to Sangerfield - just for fun. They could buy special half-fare tickets for $.05. Dad would have to type out the special tickets using one finger typing. He got sick of typing the tickets. Dad would say, 'Typing these tickets is getting to be a joke.'

Barnes also remembered that the kids roller skated around the concrete platform of the station and Collins would stop the kids from skating. Mary Margaret Welch, formerly of Waterville, told Pauline Barnes, "When he said stop-we stopped. I was scared to death of him."

"Kids used to slide down Livingstone Hill on Upper Putnam Street and across the tracks, Barnes explained. Dad would let them slide until a train was due. Then he would say. "One more slide because a train is coming.' And the kids stopped sliding.

Jeanette Collins Doyle, Pauline's sister, said that her father became ill in 1957 and never returned to work. Walter Collins passed away that year and was replaced by Jack Heenan. "My father never collected a day of retirement pay," Jeanette Doyle added.

Theodore "Ted" Jackson of East Syracuse, NY, is a retired station and telegraph operator who worked as an extra at several locations along the Utica Division from 1929-1940. After 1940 he worked on the Syracuse Division of the DL&W RR and in the tower in Chenango Forks controlling the gates and lights at crossings. Jackson also worked part-time as a trackman for my uncle, Fred Julian. Jackson also recalled the troop trains that transported National Guard units from Pennsylvania and New Jersey to Pine Camp (Fort Drum).

Jackson worked as an extra telegrapher in Hubbardsville when my father was section foreman there in 1929. He recalled the following:

…The farmers would bring in peas and beans to be shipped by Railway Express to New York City. These vegetables had been picked by migrant laborers in the Hubbardsville and Poolville area. I received a commission on Railway Express shipments, the agents did not get a commission on regular freight shipments. The Railway Express Agency was owned by all of the railroads. It was the equivalent of UPS today. The passenger train usually had a dedicated car for Railway Express that was set up in front of the mail car.

THE SIGNAL MAINTAINER

At one time, train traffic control on the Utica Division required the block system whereby tall structures of cement and metal signal blocks were located at specific intervals on one or both sides of the track or at the end of passing sidings. At the end of passing sidings two structures were placed opposite one another and near the top of each block signal extended a pointed three foot arm with red and green reflectors. When a train approached a certain point on the track, the arm on the signal block rose indicating a train was in the vicinity. To the section gang and train traffic in general, if the arm was extended upward, it meant a train was coming and they had better not have their track car on the tracks. Also, the tracks had to be secure and safe from train collisions. As mentioned earlier, section foremen carried portable phones on the track cars. Whenever necessary, wires were connected with Western Union lines on the rights of way. The section foremen then obtained information on train traffic. The location and whereabouts of the trains was of the utmost importance. Of course, passenger trains ran on schedule unless they were late as they sometimes were. For various reasons such as mechanical, trains had to wait on passing sidings until other trains arrived. At certain places on the tracks there are insulated joints with special fittings required for the block system and for bells, lights, and gates at grade crossings to function. The installation of wet cell batteries and a network of wiring near the crossings are also necessary for the automatic gates, lights, and bells.

The signal department of the railroad was responsible for keeping the block system and crossing safety equipment operating safely. It had its own Signal Maintainers Union separate from the Maintenance of Way Union. The signal maintainers repaired and maintained these signal blocks, ensuring the proper functioning of the bells, lights and automatic crossing gates at the grade crossings.

Working in the section gang during the 1940's, I occasionally observed the duties of Edward Coan and Harry Wilde. When we worked with other section gangs, I had met Bill Messenger and Fred Dean who were from the Norwich, NY area.

One of my brothers, Anthony, worked first as a section hand and then as a signal maintainer. Tony worked on the main line at New Milford, PA, on the Syracuse Division and also on the Utica Division..

There were many times when malfunctioning flasher lights or bells called out the signal maintainers. The noise from the malfunctioning bells that sometimes lasted for a lengthy time, often annoyed the local residents. They called to get the signalmen out. Sometimes when they could not be reached then my father would check the problem and try to stop the bells from ringing until the signalmen arrived. The maintenance of this equipment was essential to the prevention of serious injury and/or fatal accidents on the railroad.

The crossing watchman controlled the gates at grade crossings and held the stop sign to stop auto traffic when trains approached. Automation removed the need for the watchman and bells, lights, and gates are now in place on these crossings. In Waterville, on the corner of White Street near the bowling alley entrance, there used to stand a green shack for the crossing watchman. Only a concrete foundation now remains. William Doyle of Waterville recalled that once there was a tower mounted on the top of the shack where the watchman sat. Lynn Williams, also of Waterville, explained that the mechanism for lowering and raising the gates were in the tower. Automatic gates led to removal of the tower and elimination of the crossing watchmen. Both Doyle and Williams stated that over the years, Frank McGlinn, Jay Snow, Frank Wrobel and Phil Yapaolo, all were watchmen there. The author also recalled Frank Wrobel and Phil Yapaolo working at the crossing, and when the railroad determined that the watchmen were no longer necessary, they went to work in the section gang as section hands. Section foremen assigned them as flagmen in the large extra gangs to flag or slow trains at either end of a work project such as installing heavier rail, raising track and replacing crossties.

Watchman's Tower-Chadwicks, NY. Manned by Henry Heidel.
Courtesy of John and Jean Heidel..

RAILROAD DAYS 99

Bales of Hops to be shipped by rail. Waterville was once the "Hop capital of the world." Building was used as a station for the Utica Chenango and Western railroad.. Postcard pictures from <u>In Days Gone By</u> Waterville Historical Society

M. H. Renkin (Marshall milk station was located at Marshall (Summit) Road grade crossing, about two and one-fourth miles north of Waterville. This was a regular stop for milk trains. Building burned in 1975. Courtesy of Lincoln Davis Museum and files of Max Townsend.

THE FARMER AND THE RAILROAD

For many years, and to some extent even today, farmers and agri-business along the Utica Division depended greatly upon the railroad. In the early days of the railroad and into the 20th century, farmers shipped large amounts of hops from warehouses located on sidetracks or passing sidings near Conger Avenue and Railroad Street (South Elmwood Avenue). The GLF,[77] a farm cooperative and a familiar sight on the railroads, benefited farmers for many years in numerous communities. Also, cattle dealers loaded at various sidings along the division. Albert McKie

---

[77] Later known as Agway.

RAILROAD DAYS

recalled that near the milk station at Hubbardsville there was a cattle chute where those cattle were delivered from West Edmeston to be shipped. Milk stations such as Dairyman League, Bordens and Sheffields were familiar sights at the railroad station stops. The Renkin Milk Station was located at the Summit Road crossing in the Town of Marshall north of Waterville.

Since it was so much cheaper to transport the huge amounts of livestock feed by rail rather than by truck, feed mills were located alongside railroad tracks. The Haxton Canning factory in Waterville that once canned peas, beans, and corn is now the Louis Gale and Son Feed and Fertilizer Company. In 1951, Louis J. Gale and Son rented the P N. Lewis Feed and Lumber Co. on Conger Avenue until acquiring and remodeling the canning factory in 1963. Box cars with 20 inch grain doors delivered loose grain to the feed companies or the GLF, to be later sold to local farmers. Newer type bulk feed cars have replaced the boxcar for feed. The present railroad, NYS&W RR, still serves Louis Gale and Son in Waterville, and I. L. Richer and Agway in Sangerfield.

Milk stations such as Dairyman's League, Bordens and Sheffields were familiar sights on the railroad station stops. The Renkin Milk Station was located at the Summit Road crossing in the Town of Marshall north of Waterville.

Near the tracks east of Osborne Avenue in Waterville, there had been a Borden's plant and later a Dairyman's League milk plant that received milk from farmers for shipping by rail to the New York City and New Jersey to be bottled. Henry Gardner, formerly of Waterville, whose father was manager of the Waterville Dairyman's League plant, remembered the following:

> ...After delivery of milk to the station, it was checked visually to make sure that it was clean of any unusual coloring, etc.. Samples were then taken to test for `the level of butterfat because farmers were paid a rate based on level of butterfat and volume. 3.2 butterfat was average. The milk was then passed through a cooling system for consistency of temperature. It was then stored in a very large thermal tank. The tanks on the rail cars were thermal, and cooled with refrigeration. Sometimes milk was placed in cans on the railcars and covered with ice.[78]

Borden Milk stations were also located at Norwich and Earlville. George Perrone of Utica said that the Unadilla Valley Railroad that ran from New Berlin, NY to Bridgewater, NY hauled milk cars to Bridgewater and the DL&W would pick them up and take them south. "That was before we had the 'Hot Shot' that would take the milk to Binghamton and meet a train on the main line for New York City, Perrone said.

For many years, the twenty-two mile Richfield Springs Branch serviced milk stations, feed, fertilizer, lumber businesses, and the GLF.

Over the years many cows were severely injured or killed. Pastures and meadow stretched all along the railroad right of way throughout the division. The railroad kept the fences repaired but

---

[78] Henry Gardner e-mail, October 2006..

cows, seemed to find their way on the tracks. Locomotives, equipped with cow catchers to prevent cows struck by a train, from getting under the engine truck wheels helped prevent derailments.

Burying the cows killed by trains became an additional unfavorable task for the section man. After burying the cows or their scattered remains were buried, the section foreman contacted the farmer and a claim form would be submitted to the claim agent. The claim agent determined how much to compensate the farmer. One time in Earlville, a farm gate had been left open and several beautiful Angus cows were killed by a freight train. Farmers were not always happy with the amount that the railroad offered to pay. At one of these burials I had my first chewing tobacco experience. Lee O'Brien and Joe Banville chewed tobacco. This must have made it easier for them to combat the smell at the scene of the mangled remains. I joined them for a chew. Lee preferred Bucko or Beech-nut brands. Beech-nut was sweeter and juicier. Joe chewed O.B. Joyful. Placing his thumb and forefinger into the bag, Joe would fill one side of his mouth with a "chew." Looking at me with a mischievous smile, he said with emphasis, "Ohhh – Be Joyful." The digging of the burial hole on the right of way would then commence.

While working for his father, Rocco, my nephew, Louis Michael Langone also remembered that before burying two heifers that had been killed by the train that Jerry Massago took out his Yaro chewing tobacco. A chew of tobacco must have helped to tolerate the grisly scene. My nephew also said that Richard Baldwin of Route 12, north of Waterville, owned the cows. Rocco, then the foreman, visited Baldwin and informed him that the Erie-Lackawanna was bankrupt and unable to compensate monetarily. Therefore, Rocco delivered Erie-Lackawanna stock to him as payment of the dead cows. Considered to have no value at that time, Baldwin surprisingly, told Louis M. years later that he had received dividends on the so called "worthless" stock. Baldwin said in 1975 that the section foreman, Rocco, had visited him and made out a claim form in that the heifers were worth $250 each. Baldwin was given two shares of Erie-Lackawanna stock marked $250 each but were non-negotiable. "Around 1994 or 1995, I received two checks for those stocks, one for $140 and another for $150. I was very surprised. That was more than the cows were worth. Later I received another check for $200 or $300." Baldwin added that it took a long time since the bankruptcy court proceedings awarded money for people injuries first. Next, payments were made for animal losses and last to material things.[79]

The author asked George Pierson, a farmer and former part-time railroad section hand, if he ever helped bury cows killed by trains. "No," he replied. I remember that five of my heifers were loose on the track and I tried to head them off and get them off the tracks. A train came along and killed three of the five. I had to

---

[79] Richard Baldwin, Phone Interview, July 16, 2004.

stand there and watch them get hit. They flew right into the air. The cows had come through the railroad right of way fence but the railroad paid me. I had a Ford tractor and trailer and a neighbor helped me. We brought two cows home and we salvaged some of the beef."

I told George I remembered one farmer who blamed my father for not being compensated enough for his cows killed by a train. The farmer approached my father one day quite angry and upset. My father sympathized but explained that the decision on how much the farmer was paid was not his responsibility and that he merely supplied the claim agent with information about the cow and the circumstances surrounding the incident. "Pop" always refused to offer any opinion to the claim agent. In telling George about my experiences helping to bury cows hit by locomotives, I mentioned how a couple of men chewed tobacco- OB Joyful and Beech-Nut. Pierson said he remembered OB Joyful, Beechnut, Redman, and Bagpipe. His dad smoked Duke's Mixture and chewed OB Joyful. He remembered a brand called Warnick & Brown that my own grandfather smoked in his pipe. "It had three grades (one, two, and three), Pierson explained. "Three was the strongest and the smoke of Warnick & Brown would fill the room and you would have to go outside because the smell was so strong you couldn't breathe."

Warnick & Brown was made in Utica, NY toward the end of the nineteenth century. According to Don Williams in his book,

The Saga of Nick Stoner, A Tale of the Adirondacks, the tobacco was "good for black flies."[80] No doubt, the tobacco smoke of Warnick & Brown helped combat the prolific mosquitoes along the Sangerfield and Chenango Rivers as they meandered beside the Lackawanna tracks.

---

[80] John Pitarresi, Utica Observer Dispatch, May 21, 2004.

RAILROAD DAYS

Louis J. Gale & Son Feed and Fertilizer Co. and former site of Haxton Canning Co. Presently served by the NYS&W RR. Canning Factory Crossing. Waterville. Photograph by author.

Gold Star Feed and Grain (formerly I.L. Richer Feed and Fertilizer and Blue Seal Richer Dairy) Sangerfield, NY. Presently served by NYS&W. Photograph by author.

MISCELLANEOUS

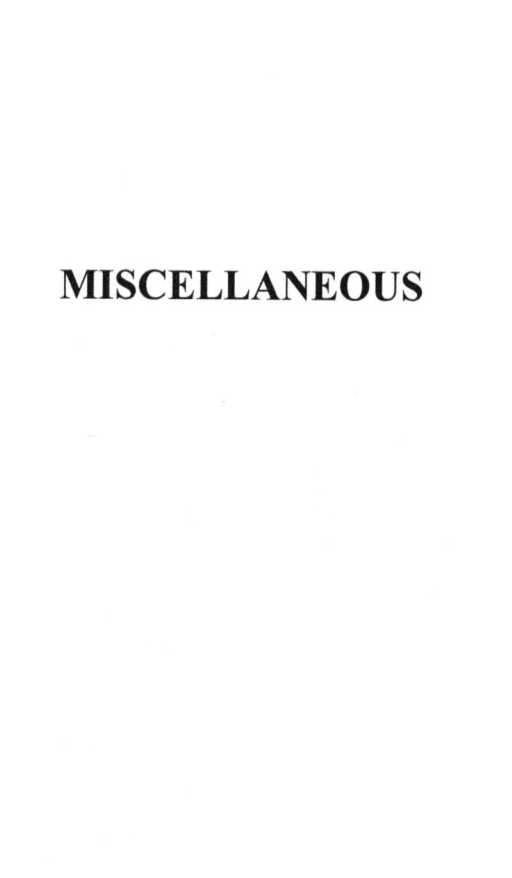

AUTO/TRAIN ACCIDENTS
AT GRADE CROSSINGS

Over the years, many accidents, sometimes fatal, have occurred at grade crossings. Hundreds have lost their lives in unfortunate encounters with locomotives. According to the History Channel, a collision occurs between a train and a car every 90 minutes. "In 2009 there were 1896 incidents at public highway rail crossings in the United States that resulted in 247 deaths and 705 injuries."[81] Despite today's technology that has been used to upgrade warning equipment, there are still many fatal auto/train accidents. A recent associated press article reported that from 2000-2004, there have been twice as many fatalities at grade crossings then fatalities from commercial plane crashes. The article further stated that on the average one person dies every day at grade crossing accidents.[82] The average freight train weighs about 12 million pounds and requires about a mile stopping distance after the emergency brakes are applied. This distance is equal to about 18 football fields.[83]

Many auto/train accidents have also occurred at the Canning Factory crossing outside the village of Waterville, NY. A

---

[81] http://safety.fhwa.dot.gov/xings/ying_facts.cfm
[82] Utica Observer Dispatch, Associated Press, July 11, 2004.
[83] www.YouTube.com/watch

double fatality occurred in 1937 when a train struck an Haxton Foods tractor trailer loaded with canned goods.

Lester Bugbee of Deansboro remembered in detail that particular accident that killed his father and a passenger.

…My father, Lester G. Bugbee, was the driver of that truck and he and the eighteen year old son of the truck owner, lost their lives. The accident occurred March 30, 1937. The truck was a 15 ton 1936 Mack tractor trailer, and it had just left the canning factory with a load of canned goods. A house on the corner that is no longer there had hindered the view at the crossing. Dick Lewis (of Waterville), whose father had a feed mill south of the crossing, heard the crash.[84]

Fatal truck/train accident-March 30, 1937. Truck carrying canned goods. Driver and passenger killed. Canning Factory crossing(site of several accidents) in Waterville.
Photograph by Minford Peterson.

---

[84] Lester M. Bugbee, Phone Interview, January 10, 2005.

Gerald Furner of Waterville who has lived near the Canning Factory crossing for many years, said that in the 1930's, a train struck a pickup truck driven by Clayton Bogan, a former resident of Waterville. Bogan was not injured. Also, Mary VanMatt Wilson, who has lived on Canning factory road for many years, recalled her father's 1952 Nash Rambler being struck by a train at the crossing. He was not injured but the bumper was damaged.[85] The author remembers that the late Dewey Nichols, while employed by the Canning Factory, had an accident at that same crossing, but he was not injured. The bumper of his pickup sustained a glancing blow as he traveled over the crossing. In 1974 an Erie-Lackawanna train demolished a car at the crossing and a woman and her baby were killed.

The author interviewed two individuals who recalled that prior to the construction of the underpass on U.S. Route 20 in the Town of Sangerfield, on June 26th, 1936 a tragic auto/train accident occurred where that road intersected with the railroad crossing. It killed six members of two families traveling from New York City in one car.

Jack Gallagher of Sangerfield recalled the accident... "The train stopped where Heckert's store was located (the site of the former Olde Poste Restaurant). My father and I went to the accident." Gallagher related. "I was about twelve years old at the

---

[85] Kasper VanMatt Phone Interview, March 16, 2005.

time and stayed in the car. My father and Royal Plante helped remove people from the car that had been struck by the train. Gallagher further explained that the cow catcher on the engine went through the car and my father said he was sick for several days after that."

Ted Jackson of East Syracuse, who at the time was working as a telegraph operator at Richfield Junction said that it was a passenger train and the engine number was 964 – a Mother Hubbard engine. The engineer was Otto Klausner and the fireman was W.R. Smith. "I heard about it from the dispatcher," said Jackson, "and I got in a friend's car and we went to Sangerfield. My grandfather, Andrew Getman, was station agent at the time at Richfield Junction. When I got to Sangerfield, the six bodies were covered and the engine had not yet been separated from the auto. It was an awful sight."

According to the <u>Waterville Times</u> of July 2, 1936, the victims were traveling from New York City and their car was demolished by a northbound passenger train. The train had left Binghamton at 5:45 A.M. An inquest was held by Coroner Dr. Gordon Holden in the office of Dr. E. Deland Battles in Waterville on the following Monday. It was determined that the train crew was not at fault. The engineer, Otto Klausner, said that the train was traveling at 45-50 miles an hour and two cars were approaching the crossing. He testified that he blew the whistle 1600 feet south of the crossing and 1100 feet south—two long-one short and two long blasts lasting until the crossing was reached. At 100 feet when it appeared that the cars were not going to stop, Klausner said that he applied the emergency brakes. The bell on the locomotive was ringing steadily and he brought the train to a stop 1,000 feet north of the crossing. A Massachusetts man was driving the car following the New York car. He said that his car and the car that was hit by the train were both traveling about 35 miles an hour and that he avoided being killed by swerving and he ran into a signal pole. A Syracuse couple was in the car following the Massachusetts man. Drivers of both cars following said they did not hear the train whistle or bell. Witnesses said that the wagging red signal and bells at the crossing were working, but the view may have been obstructed by a row of elm trees. The newspaper article further reported that the Town of Sangerfield Board suggested that the State put a stop sign at the intersection of Routes 12 and 20. They said it might have prevented the accident if a stop sign were there. (A stop sign was not erected at the intersection until an automobile/Greyhound Bus accident killed a Pennsylvania family in 1946 at the intersection of Routes 12 and 20).

In 1939 work got underway for the construction of the underpass that eliminated the grade crossing where the accident had occurred.

114 LOUIS C. LANGONE

Sangerfield, NY. Rt. 20 R.R. crossing before underpass construction ca. 1938

Route 20 grade crossing appearance at time of fatal accident June26, 1936. Photo by Minford Peterson. Courtesy of Ronald Foppes.

RAILROAD DAYS

Construction of Route 20 overpass on 1939 in the Town of Sangerfield. Auto/passenger - train accident in 1936 killed six members of family. Photo by Theodore Jackson.

Dana Cross Broedel of North Brookfield, NY, said that her uncle, an auto mechanic, was killed in an accident at the Swamp Road crossing in 1925 in North Brookfield where the old station stood previously. Having just repaired a car, and enroute to deliver it to the owner, Cross's uncle found himself stalled on the tracks and struck by a passing train.

Sangerfield, NY Rt. 20 R.R. crossing during underpass construction, ca. 1938

Route 20 Overpass at Sangerfield, NY - 2005. Top phoro by Minford Peterson

Inside section 69 tool house. Names on wall refer to: Louie(Langone), Sr., Lee(O'Brien), Ernie(Clemens),, Joe (Banville), John(Giedritis), and Phil(Yapaolo.- November 18, 1944. Courtesy of Robert Cross (presently restoring the tool house) and Dana Broedel. Photograph by author.

NORTH BROOKFIELD-SECTION GANG HEADQUARTERS 1940's

During World War II Jack Heenan served as the station agent at North Brookfield, later succeeding Walter Collins in that post in Waterville. Worth Warner of North Brookfield reminded me that Jack used to take care of the boiler in the pump house next to the water tank that was full of water for the locomotives. Jack would feed pea coal to the boiler so that the steam would be maintained to pump water from the well for the tank. Ernie Clemens told me that he helped to take the wooden water tank down several years ago.

North of the Swamp Road crossing in North Brookfield, and across from my father's railroad tool house stood the Charles Kling Mills. George Pierson explained that hopper type railroad cars loaded with coal would be parked on the sidetrack over a pit. Coal would be released between the tracks from the hopper down into a pit and a conveyer belt would transport the coal up a chute into the silos that stored the coal for later delivery.

Lucien Neff, who also worked about two years in the extra gang after the War remembers working for Kling Mills unloading railroad cars. He recalls that if they were not unloaded in three days, demurrage fee would be charged.

Every year my father bought tons of coal from Charlie Kling to burn in our coal furnace. Kling Mills also received livestock feed from the railroad cars and 'Pop" purchased feed for our pigs and chickens from there. Once in a while we also raised a cow. It was common to see businesses along the railroad that sold coal, livestock feed, and lumber. The building that once housed a milk station still stands next to the Swamp Road crossing at North Brookfield.

Donald Larkin's brother, Richard worked for my father during World War II. Don's wife, Esther, recalls riding the train during the war while in nurse's training at the former Memorial Hospital in Utica. From the hospital she took the bus to New Hartford and boarded the train for North Brookfield and returned the same way. She enjoyed the scenery from the train, especially around Cassville. "The views were not the same as from the road," stated Mary Lillie Raffauf, whose father had a store not far from the railroad tracks, remembered how she used to love to hear the sound of the train whistle.

North Brookfield-Summer of 1951. The station was located close to the corner of Swamp Road. Order board attached to station to inform trains of a train order. One arm for north bound and one for south bound trains. Arms rose automatically to a horizontal position by station agent to signal trainmen. Agent attached order to a forked wire hook to be snared by one of the trainmen. Marian and Barbara Jackson standing in front of car. Collection of Theodore Jackson.

RAILROAD DAYS 121

North Brookfield Station and Water tank that once provided water for countless steam locomotives. Pump house with coal boiler is adjacent to tank. A well provided the water for the tank and for section men for many years. 1951. Collection of Theodore Jackson

Left to Right- Jack Heenan- Station agent at North Brookfield(later at Waterville), Andrew J. Getman. Photo by Theodore Jackson, 1951. Getman was station operator at Hubbardsville when author's father was section foreman there in 1929.

NYSW&W Railway Gondola freight cars loaded with railroad crossties in Waterville-2003. In the 1940's gondolas that carried crossties were unloaded by hand on the Utica Division from "gons" parked on sidetracks or from a work train as directed by the section foreman. Photograph by author.

THE WORK TRAIN

Gondola and/or hopper type cars plus the locomotive and caboose made up the work train. The major work projects along the division, such as laying heavier rail, replacing ties, and raising track several inches, occasionally required the presence of a work train. Work trains with gondola cars transported rails, kegs of spikes, and angle bars (for connecting the rail joints), alongside the right of way for future use. The section men unloaded ties and other materials such as tie plates from the gondola cars. Section men picked up the scrap and threw it onto the gondola cars as the train moved along. When rails were being picked up the Kohring Crane was also part of the work train.

My favorite job was picking up scrap and tossing it up and into the gondola. "Pop" always said I could get dirtier than anyone else doing this. Work trains brought numerous hopper cars loaded with cinders for ballast, needed when the tracks were raised. Sometimes I sat on the top of the hopper cars and used a long pole-like bar to poke cinders down toward the tracks. The section foreman walked the right of way directing the engineer to advance the train or back it up as needed. A firm grip on the end of the car prevented us from falling off and I do not recall anyone falling. Sometimes I was on the ground attaching pans so the cinders would move to the side. Pans were located on both sides of the hopper and an occasional tap with a spiking hammer on the side of the car would increase the flow of the cinders. Some cinders fell into the center of the track and later we manned shovels to spread the cinders. The cinders would flow from the hoppers all day providing ballast needed when the tracks were raised several inches. The average raise was 6".

Whenever a passenger or freight train was due, the work train ceased operation and proceeded to the nearest passing siding to wait for the scheduled train to pass. The section hands stayed busy leveling cinders or doing some other temporary work not hindering train traffic.

Needless to say, unloading cinders was a dirty job. Sometimes a cinder entered the eye. The first aid kit always had an eye cup to be filled with boric acid and water for an eye wash. A cinder or two in the eye occurred often. I recall that when a train would speed by "Pop" advised us to look in the direction that the train is going to minimize the chance of acquiring a cinder in the eye.

By the 1950's, with the introduction of the diesel locomotives on the Utica Division, cinders for ballast became scarce. Work trains transported hopper cars loaded with crushed stone to be used as ballast. Ron Furner recalled that one time while he was on top of a hopper pushing stone down, he lost his footing and slid right down the steel floor of the hopper and passed out of the train right through the pan that was attached to the bottom of the hopper.

We would look forward to the end of the day when we returned to the tool house and to that nice old well with the cold drinking water at North Brookfield. In addition to the refreshing cold water, the old well also provided an opportunity to remove some of the grime from our face and hands before going home.

Sangerfield in 1941 in vicinity of Chernoff farm. Snow plow work train in operation after large snowstorm in March. Louis Langone Sr. in foreground. Photograph by Minford Peterson. Collection of author.

WINTER ON THE RAILROAD

In wintertime "section hand" railroad work could be cold, uncomfortable, and adventurous. In 1917, Grandfather Rocco was a section foreman, and under him, my father, who had worked as a trackman at that time, related to the author the story of a passenger train getting stuck in the snow in North Bridgewater at Babcock Hill. Dominic Langone (not related) and "Pop" were in

Sauquoit and had to ride a snowplow connected to two locomotives to Babcock Hill.

...We put snow in the boiler of the locomotive that was stuck to get water for it. We would shovel for an hour and get only a gallon of water – not enough to get steam. We kept the engines low to prevent them from heating up. The train that was stuck was across from the cemetery. We worked all day until the next night and had no lunch. We were paid straight time since there was no time and one-half back then. The baggage man of the train, Frank Gates, got ice cream and we ate ice cream and bread that night. A farmer by the name of Burt Brown came over with 20 gallon cans of water. He had us all over for breakfast and the roadmaster told Brown to feed everyone and the railroad would pay him. Bacon was served a foot high with sausage and eggs. He fed over twenty that day. Another crew came on later. We had over 100 men and we succeeded in shoveling the train out. Sometimes the snowplow got stuck. There were no spreaders on the plows. I was 15 years old at the time.

What was it like to work on the tracks along a mile long open cut,[86] (or on one of the long sidetracks) with snow flying around and the wind howling, the temperature at or below 0°? And what was it like when it was 25° and trackmen shoveled tons of snow from the side tracks? Or when switches needed sweeping, or when switches and grade crossings required removal of ice with pick axes. After the ice was chopped away, the men spread rock salt so the wheel flange could travel along the rails safely without the possibility of derailment.

---

[86] Cut- where the right of way is cut through a hill, slope, or knoll.

Ron Furner related how keeping the flange of he rails open has changed over the years:

…We don't worry anymore about cleaning crossings in the winter. The locomotives seem to handle it. One time when we were working on a double track in a crossing, we took out the old black top from one track and let it lay across the other. Because of bad communication between the foreman and the engineer of an oncoming train, we were surprised when a train came along without our being prepared for it. The Amtrak train just plowed right through it.

In summer, tamping ballast under the cross-ties at various low spots in the track, was necessary to keep the track level and smooth so that the passenger trains traveled in relative comfort over the rails. Also, rough track contributed to broken rails and derailments. When the ground froze tamping cinder ballast under the ties (to keep the track fairly smooth) was out of the question. Therefore, the section men temporarily placed thin wooden shims under the tie plates as support after the track was raised and leveled.

Ernest Clemens pointed out some of the commands from the foreman to the jack man. "Joint ahead and quarter back," as the section foreman supervised the raising of the track. I remember other commands such as– "Joint ahead or center back." The same ones were used in the lining of track with the lining bars.

In the winter, the men positioned snow fences along the right of way in various locations such as the long cuts or open areas where the wind and snow caused huge accumulations of snow on the tracks.

March 19, 1941, there was a big snowstorm and train #832 –the Utica to Norwich "local" (southbound), got stuck in Sangerfield just north of the former Chernoff farm. The "Hotshot" freight and passenger train #816 was held in Waterville. It backed up to Richfield Junction and got on the Y so that the engine could head the right way going back to Utica. The "Hotshot" out of Utica connected with the main line "Hotshot" at Binghamton. The #803 train was held at Hubbardsville.[87] Theodore Jackson relieved Walter Collins in Waterville on that day at 8 P.M. He recalled that Walt Collins hung around a while after being relieved and invited Jackson to stay at Collins' home after finishing his shift the next morning at 5 A.M.

In the winter, extra men hired in addition to the regular men, shoveled now in the sidings and when the snowplow train came through. George Kelley recalled Bill Doyle breaking a few shovels. Kelley said, "Your father warned him," by saying, 'Doyle, don't break any more shovels.' The author also

---

[87] Theodore Jackson Personal Interview, July 7, 2004.

remembered that day and reminded Bill about this. "That snow was heavy," Doyle replied with a huge grin.

I will always remember shoveling snow at the siding at the crossing where the Paris railroad station was located. Looking south from the Lincoln Davies lumber and old coal yard on the west side of the tracks, I saw a freight train coming toward us from the direction of the Renkin milk station at Marshall on Summit Road. I watched the steam locomotive chug and puff as the wheels gave a familiar spinning sound and huge amounts of black and gray smoke unfurling back lazily from the stack and roll upward and over the cab. As it approached the crossing where we had been shoveling snow, the contrast of the smoke and black of the locomotive and the white steam against the very white snow and by the clear blue sky, created a beautiful scene (unfortunately, I had no camera). The diesel surpasses the steam engine in power (to pull the big freight trains up Paris Hill) but they would never duplicate that picturesque winter scene many years ago at Paris Station.

Ronald Jones, owner of Lincoln-Davies at Paris Station recalled a time when a train that had a cattle car loaded with cows was stuck in the snow down by the lumber yard. Since the train had been stuck for a while, the train crew came up to the store and asked for help. The cows in the cattle car needed milking. Merritt Wooden, one of the store employees helped milk the cows. Jones explained that after the cows were milked, Wooden returned to the store, "While Merritt was standing around talking, he reached into his back pocket for a chew of tobacco. Instead of tobacco, Merritt pulled out a handful of manure," Jones related with a big laugh. The working area must have been quite limited milking the cows on the cattle car.

Ernest Clemens tells a story about working on the snowplow train. One winter he was with an assistant roadmaster named Dominic.[88] (Author's note-probably Dominic Simielo from Syracuse).

...I was asked if I thought I could handle the snowplow. So with much patience while I learned, I thought I could handle the snowplow. I was temporarily transferred to that responsibility on those frigid winter days. It was warm up there in the plow. The plow was pushed by the engine and I handled the wings at crossings, bridges and elsewhere. One time[89] when the wind and drifting snow plugged a section of the track south of Waterville and Sangerfield, I was with the plow and a backhoe type of equipment was called to remove the snow and free the stuck train in the vicinity of Route 20 near the Chernoff crossing.

Clemens also remembered the men working in sub-zero temperatures when it was often necessary to wear felt boots to keep the feet protected from the cold. When the weather was too severe, we retreated to the tool house and the comfort of the wood stove to keep warm.

---

[88] Probably Dominic Simielo(sp.?) from Syracuse.
[89] March, 19, 1941.(Theodore Jackson Interview, July 7, 2004).

Robert Masca, a retired section foreman from Waterville said that when he was a section man there were many nights in the winter they didn't make it home because of having to work around the clock removing snow. "There was a time on Christmas Day I got called out. With three little boys at home – that was hard."

"Ice on the tracks was always a problem, especially at crossings," John Swald, a former conductor recalled. "One time on the Blue Line, I saw your brother, Rocco, working with his men at a crossing. It was so cold- your brother's ears and nose were all red and I think frozen."

Roger Nichols said the snow at Shimel's Cut near Huxtables' farm in South Columbia, was so heavy that engines would get stuck over there. "Lots of times in the winter, the train had to go to Richfield Springs because a propane car for Suburban Gas was needed there.

Paris Hill in the winter has always been another world. When Bob Masca was a foreman, he recalled sending the gang to Paris to sweep snow from switches while he rode up in the engine of a train to check crossings. Arriving at one end of Green's crossing going about 20 miles an hour, he heard the engineer say, 'Hang on!" The engine became airborne and ended up in the creek. One of the cars uncoupled and started down the hill towards Cassville. Fortunately, it did not reach any crossings in Cassville. Since there was drifting snow, the car stopped after six or eight car lengths, Masca recalled.

Masca said that one time, before he became a foreman, he and Jerry Massago were to ride the snowplow to Richfield Springs.

…We got as far as Bridgewater and the plow went on the ground and we spent 10 hours putting the plow back on the tracks. It was cold and rainy that day. Back then, we worked 16 hour days and Jerry and I stayed at a motel near West Winfield. The next morning we were back working on the plow and finally got it on the move.

Masca also indicated that another time after a snowstorm, he and Massago went on the plow to Richfield Springs. After reaching South Columbia, (three miles from Richfield Springs) he said the plow hit a drift 8-10 feet high.

…It stopped us dead in our tracks. The engineer told us to close the wings so we could back up and try again. So we braced our feet for the impact. This time we buried the plow and had to crawl out the top window of the plow.

Masca described Jerry Massago of Barneveld as an "old-timer" on the railroad. As he related his times on the snow plow with Massago, Masca indicated his admiration for him. "He taught me a lot and he was a good man. At times Jerry was an assistant foreman and had also filled in at times as foreman."

Ron Furner recalled that the snowplow or Jordan Spreader[90] was followed by the engine and the caboose. "Today there is a snowplow on each end with the engine in the middle," he added. Making it possible to plow in both directions as needed..

---

[90] Jordan Spreader- Equipped with wings for plowing snow. Also used to dress the roadbed in summer.

RAILROAD DAYS   133

Shimel's Cut . Often a major snow problem in the winter on the Richfield Springs Branch due to wind from the northwest. Snowplow is clearing the tracks of snow during the winter of 1972-73. George Brill, head mechanic of the Utica and Syracuse Divisions and Ronald

The DL&W tracks on the left of station about 1910. Unadilla Valley tracks on right. Photo from <u>Days along the Buckwheat and Dandelion</u> by Fred Pugh

Bridgewater station on the Richfield Springs branch in the early 20th century. Constructed in 1904, the station was shared by both the DL&W and the Unadilla Valley RR. Milk trains from New Berlin made connections with the DL&W at Bridgewater. Courtesy of Fran Combar, Harry Lenz, and the Bridgewater Historical Society.

THE RICHFIELD SPRINGS BRANCH

One of the major spurs of the old Delaware Lackawanna and Western Railroad (later known as Erie-Lackawanna) extended from Richfield Junction (near Cassville) to Richfield Springs. The Utica Chenango and Susquehanna Valley Railroad constructed this branch between 1869 and 1870, which later became a branch of the Utica Division of the DL&W RR. The original plan, which did not materialize, was to build tracks all the way to New York City by way of Richfield Springs, Cooperstown, Colliersville, and the Catskills.[91]

According to eighty-six year old Doris Huxtable, lifetime resident of Millers Mills, and historian for the Town of Columbia, a representative of the Utica Chenango and Susquehanna Valley Railroad came to the farm from Boston in 1868. The railroad was seeking a right of way and wanted to run the line through the David Youngs property, which became the Huxtable farm in Millers Mills). In 1868 a contract was drawn up giving the railroad the right of way.

Where the railroad crossed the road at the Youngs property, the railroad timetable listed it as Youngs Crossing.. From that time on, Youngs Crossing became a household phrase.[92]

After 50 years of dealing with horse drawn carts on muddy and snowbound rural paths, the Youngs were to be connected with the outside world by the steam engine. The train ran through the center of the farm, a mere 100 feet from the main house.[93]

Jack Huxtable also explained how David Youngs, who had made an agreement with the railroad, wrote the following in his diary of 1870: "Railroad gravel train reached here (Millers Mills) in P.M...."[94] Huxtable said that this meant the railroad footing

---

[91] William C. Kessler, The Railroad Age in Madison County, p. 19
[92] John Huxtable, "Train Service to Youngs Crossing," E-Mail dated November 11, 2004.
[93] Ibid.
[94] Ibid.

was underway and trackmen were laying the initial rails. When Youngs deeded the land in 1869 he charged only one dollar for the use of the land. However, he requested a flag stop at the farm whenever anyone in the family requested a ride. A stone loading platform was set up in an attempt to establish a regular station stop at Young's Crossing. The railroad listed Young's crossing in the timetable but it never became a scheduled station stop.

The railroad had a significant effect on Young's' Dairy Knife business. Another diary entry by Young's is as follows:

"Sent several boxes of knives by railroad to West Winfield. The largest amount of knives sent off this week even amounted to $1,000." Another entry in the diary is dated May 28th and reads as follows:...*"First train of passenger coaches went through to Richfield Springs."*[95]

Doris Huxtable also stated that there was an agreement with the railroad. "If anyone in the Huxtable family wanted to ride the train, all that the family member had to do was wave a white handkerchief and the train would have to stop."

At the western terminus, just south of where the depot at Richfield Junction station was located, the main tracks of the Utica Division connected with the Richfield Springs Branch where a wye is still located making it possible to turn a train or railroad car around. The north leg of the wye was referred to as the Richfield

---

[95] Ibid.

Main and trains from Utica would switch to this leg and proceed to Richfield Springs.

George Perrone, a retired conductor of the DL&W and Erie Lackawanna Railroad, born in Richfield Springs, said that years ago a switch tender was employed at the Junction, and all he did was work the switches - keeping in contact with the station operator.

Perrone said that there was also a wye at the Richfield Springs end of the spur.

...A train would pull into the station on Lake Street, load up and do its turning on the way out. The train would back up to put the engine in the right direction. One leg of the wye went all the way to the lake. In the early 1920's cakes of ice were cut out of Canadarago Lake that furnished all of the DL&W RR. Boxcars would be loaded with ice and shipped to various locations including Chenango Forks and Utica where ice would be stored in icehouses. There was also a roundhouse at one time at Richfield Springs but it was not round. It looked more like a barn and it housed one engine and it was located near Bronner Street. Floyd Dibble was the fireman who kept the engine fired up all night. In the morning, the engine would hook up with a milk car at Richfield Springs, collect other milk cars at milk stations along the "Branch," and haul them to Richfield Junction to make connections with a freight going to Binghamton, and then to New York City. Empty cars would be left for the next day's milk cans. It was an education just to see the milk cans loaded onto the car and placed in a perfectly neat order. This was during the 1920's and part of the 1930's. A special train crew lived at Richfield Springs and manned the milk train. The crew was hired just for that train and was not subject to seniority union rules. Some of the train crewmembers were Stan Osterhout, Harold Barber, and George Penner. This lasted until the thirties and then milk cars and creamery cars became part of the freight trains that came from Utica.[96]

In a serpentine fashion, the tracks of the "Branch" wound its way for 22 miles, passing over many grade crossings and three main highways – Routes 20, 8 and 51. The trains rolled through rich farmland that produced potatoes, hops, beans, corn and wheat. For more than a hundred years, it served the picturesque rural communities of Cassville, Bridgewater, West Winfield, Cedarville Station (Chepachet), Millers Mills, South Columbia and Richfield Springs. This short branch once carried whole families on Sundays to the health springs of Richfield Springs and to Canadarago Lake and Park. Freight trains transported milk from the milk stations, and delivered boxcars and hopper cars of livestock feed to Schoonmaker's Feed Company, J. Stanley Watkin's, and the G.L.F. (Agway) in West Winfield. Also, the freight trains carried carloads of cowhides to Hiteman Leather in West Winfield, lumber and coal for the Welch's, gondola coal cars to Roscoe Shimel in South Columbia, and tanker cars of propane gas to Suburban Gas in Richfield Springs.

With the exception of Bridgewater and Cedarville (Chepachet), the depots of the "Branch" have all disappeared. "People would come from all over just to see the Cedarville station building. Probably because of the way it was built and painted. It

---

[96] George Perrone Interview with Louis C. Langone, September 28, 2004

was recognized as one of the nicest."[97] For a time it was converted into a restaurant and named "Petticoat Junction."

In 1938, the speed limit for first class and freight trains was 35 miles an hour and engines of the 500, 700, and 900 classes were restricted to 15 miles an hour.[98] In later years, it would be necessary to reduce the speed considerably.

Miller's Mills Depot – 1929. Passenger train approaching Millers Mills station. Earl Gay, a long time resident of Millers Mills told Doris Huxtable that at one time six to seven trains (passenger and milk) traveled the "Branch." Courtesy of Doris Huxtable, Town of Columbia historian.

---

[97] George Perrone, Interview with Louis C. Langone, September 28, 2004.
[98] DL&WRR Timetable #76 dated 1938, p.61.

The DL&W delivered milk and other freight to Bridgewater for further shipment by the Unadilla Valley Railroad, a 20 mile railroad route extending from Bridgewater to New Berlin.

The Unadilla Valley produced large amounts of milk and milk cans would be brought to Leonardsville and the Valley Forks, loaded on the train and then brought to Bridgewater for the DL&W to transport. The DL&W and Unadilla Valley shared the same station in Bridgewater and the UV tracks were located to the right of the station. The Unadilla Valley RR closed down in 1960.[99]

Perrone said another railroad – actually a trolley line, known as the Southern New York, serviced Richfield Springs. It paralleled Lake Street and crossed at the Lake House. There was a transfer track that connected that railroad with the DL&WRR. The Southern New York went from Mohawk to Richfield Springs and to Oneonta.

Winter on the "Branch" often created problems for train traffic. Roger Nichols of Waterville, while working for the Erie-Lackawanna, said that due to the great amount of snow that filled Shimel's Cut in the area of South Columbia, the locomotives would get stuck. "Lots of times in the winter the train had to go to Richfield Springs because a propane car for the Propane Gas Co. was needed there." David Robertson, who resides near Shimel's

---

[99] D. Tanney(Ed.) <u>Remembered Years</u>, Story of the Unadilla Valley by Ralph Gustin. .p. 153-156

Cut, said that the roadbed, is still owned by the NY Susquehanna RR, but is leased to the Snowtoppers Snowmobile Club from McCoon Road to Richfield Springs. "The snow is still a problem for the snowmobiles since the wind from the northwest is fierce and snow still fills the cut at times."[100]

As opposed to the main line of the Utica Division that was equipped with 80 pound rail to the yard (and later in the 1940's, changed to 105 pound to the yard), the "Branch" mostly had 75 pound. rail. For many years, the older style screw spikes, rather than cut spikes, kept the rails in place. Screw spikes required a specific T shaped wrench for removing the spikes. Long claw bars removed cut spikes.

Speed of the trains on the "Branch" was more restricted. According to a 1938 timetable, speed on the "Branch" varied from 10 miles per hour to 35 miles per hour. Speed was restricted based on location, curves, bridges, grade crossings, city streets and size of engines.[101]

Over the years as the railroad endured hard times, which required extending the length of the sections. Consequently, maintenance became more difficult. Lack of money definitely contributed to the terrible condition of the tracks on the "Branch."

---

[100] David Robertson, Personal Interview, September 27, 2004.
[101] DL&WRR Timetable, No. 76, 1938.

As the condition of the tracks deteriorated, railroad officials reduced speed limit to 10 miles an hour.[102] "We did an inspection patrol every Friday and riding on the tracks was like riding on a roller coaster. There wasn't a lot of freight business on the "Branch" in the early 1970's, and I remember that when we patrolled, we would eat lunch in the stands at the Livestock Auction at East Winfield," Nichols recalled.

Ed Luther, a retired brakeman, said that when the trains traveled on the "Branch" the cars would sway and roll from side to side. To ride the "Branch" by motorcar or high railer, was riding through a forest as the brush whipped along the sides of the vehicles traveling along the tracks.

In the early part of the 20th century, Joseph Perrone and my grandfather, Rocco Langone, were section foremen on the "Branch." From 1930-1975, Rocco Tofalo of West Winfield, my uncle Fred Julian, my father, Louis Sr., and my brother, Rocco, each took their turn as section foreman on the "Branch."

Considering the "Branch" a money loser, the Erie-Lackawanna sold it to the Delaware and Otsego Railroad in 1973, and incorporated it as the Central New York Railway (CNYK).[103] In 1997, a Delaware and Otsego subsidiary, the New York Susquehanna and Western Railroad, took it over permanently.[104]

---

[102] Erie-Lackawanna Railway Timetable, No. 3, 1971.
[103] Scot Hatley, Delaware Otsego Story, Trains, January 1988, p. 30.
[104] Bill Stephens, The Susie-Q Saga, Trains, January 1998, p.42.

About two miles of track from Richfield Junction to North Bridgewater is all that remains of this railroad spur, since the tracks between Richfield Junction and Richfield Springs were removed a few years ago. The remainder of the old spur is about 19.4 miles of narrow cinder packed pathway covered in places with weeds, grass, and thick brush on the right of way. Some portions are being used as a recreational trail for hikers and snowmobiles.

Whenever I travel Route 20 by car going through Bridgewater, East Winfield, South Street in West Winfield, Hackley Street near the rear of the old Clarodin Restaurant, I observe the cinder pathway where the tracks once stretched. The roadbed in some places is almost completely concealed by the trees and the brush, and I reflect on what once was—when trains transported the milk, the coal, the other freight, cattle and cowhides – and the countless passengers - through the bucolic hills and valleys of the Route 20 countryside of Central New York.

I reminisce on those railroad days of long ago on the "Branch," when during my summer vacations, I enjoyed the scenic open-air ride back and forth to and from work on board the old track car or from my seat inside the high railer (Vehicle equipped to travel on the highway or the railway).

Richfield Junction – Curving to right of main track is the South end of the Wye that connected to former Richfield Branch. Milepost 273(Miles from Hoboken, NJ- eastern terminal of the DL&W and Erie-Lackawanna RR.

Poolville Pond. Milepost 255- the approximate end of the Nine Mile Swamp and section 69. The next section in the 1940's extended south twelve miles and supervised by section foreman, John Cursh who was headquartered at Sherburne, NY. Photograph by Steve Callanen.

NINE MILE SWAMP

The Nine Mile Swamp extends south of Sangerfield, NY to the vicinity of Poolville Pond near Poolville, NY. For many years, around the middle of the nineteenth century, the notorious outlaws and horse thieves, the Loomis Gang homesteaded on the western edge of the swamp. Now, the years and the clearing of land for pastures and meadows have taken a toll on the swamp. It is not as dense as it once was in the 19th century, and the notorious Loomis Gang of the swamp is long gone, never having robbed a train. I first heard of the Loomis Gang when my father pointed out the tree on the old homestead on Mason Road where local vigilantes attempted to hang Plumb Loomis.[105]

The railroad passes through the swamp, and time has not altered the elements under which the railroaders had to labor. The 7,000 acre tract is actually eleven miles in length and originally about a mile wide.[106] (Probably calculated from Route 12 to the western edge where Swamp Road is located and where the Loomis Gang had their homestead). Two creeks flow through the Swamp. Railroad ties and fence posts were made from timber from the swamp.[107]

After loading up with water at the well that was near the big water tank, the track car headed down the track before arriving at the worksite. The car was then removed from the track at one of the takeoffs (made out of two railroad ties). A special turntable device would be used to swing the car off the rails. Sometimes the car would be removed at a grade crossing. Two men would stand on the front of the car to lift it from the rails and then push it off

---

[105] Neighbors wanted to end the Loomis menace. Plumb survived the hanging, but Loomis' did move away.
[106] Norman Cowen, (Town of Sangerfield historian), Nine Mile Swamp, 1947.
[107] Ibid.

the crossing into a safe area. If working near North Brookfield, Hubbardsville or Poolville stations where side tracks were available, the car would be parked on the siding.

Railroad work in the Nine Mile Swamp was unique in several ways. The railroad is reputed to be the hottest place in the summer and the coldest in the winter. Working in the swamp in July and August was, to say the least, very uncomfortable; hot, muggy and mosquito infested. At times, summer days became so hot one could see heat waves quivering back and forth above the tracks. Track workers always enjoyed rainy days since work ceased and poker games commenced.

The railroad assumed the responsibility of repairing fences along the right of way walking through many wet areas and an occasional sink hole or bog hole. One time Bill Hickey stepped into one up to his neck. When asked about the incident, he said he could not remember stepping into a bog or waterhole while fixing fence in the Nine Mile Swamp. I had remembered it. If it had been me with my short stature, I would have been submerged. Once in a while, snakes and bees nesting in kegs of spikes that had been placed at intervals along the right of way caused some very fast moves.

By mid-morning, the section hands began to feel the intense heat with our shirts soaked with sweat. Old timers (who seldom appeared to perspire) never rolled up their sleeves or removed their shirts. Only the young and reckless removed their shirts, which resulted in sunburns for that generation. By the end of the summer everyone had a deep tan. By the end of the day, sweat and cinders combined to create the inevitable – very dirty men.

Returning to North Brookfield we would stop at the well for a drink. Often I thought of the Sons of the Pioneers song from the cowboy movies, "Cool Water."

Schuyler Street-West Utica. Trains of the NYS&W Railway Co. continue to travel down the middle of the street at a speed limit of eight miles an hour.

SCHUYLER STREET

The summer of 1948 turned out to be my last summer on the railroad until college. My father supervised the large extra gang and that season's project was to raise the track and replace ties on Schuyler Street in West Utica. Schuyler Street is about three-fourths of a mile long with houses close to the track. Though there are fewer trains today, they still travel slowly down the street.[108] The 150 pound girder rails extend down the middle of

---

[108] The 1971 Erie-Lackawanna No. 3 timetable indicated eight miles an hour on Utica city streets including Schuyler Street.(Page 90.)

the street and measure nine inches high from the tie plate to the asphalt. The angle bars used diagonally at the joints to connect the rails use 12 bolts with six on either side. One hundred and five pound rail use only six bolts.[109]

To work on a city street with the railroad running down the middle of it was an experience. There was traffic from automobiles, trains, and pedestrians. The houses are located fairly close together.

Located near the end of Schuyler Street is West End Brewing Company, (now known as the F.X. Matt Brewing Company) manufacturer of Utica Club, Matt and Saranac beer, in addition to other miscellaneous beverages. In 1948, West End brewed only Utica Club ale and lager. The Fort Schuyler Brewery was West End's local competitor and Matt and Saranac were beers of the future. West End was always generous with free samples of beer in their taproom where they tapped sample barrels. Raising the track on Schuyler Street provided an enjoyable change from working in other areas, especially compared to July and August in the Nine Mile Swamp.

Before raising the track, some bad ties needed replacing. Since there was curbing at the end of the ties, the ties could not be

---

[109] Robert Masca, Personal Interview., January 20, 2004.

pulled out lengthwise, but had to be twisted and they came out at an angle.[110]

To raise the track and force crushed stone ballast under the ties, it was first necessary to break up the blacktop with jack hammers. A large air compressor machine, kept on the job for this powered the jack hammers used for breaking up blacktop and for digging and tamping ballast. Gerry Furner remembered how Bill Jannone who lived in Waterville, would rush to work so he could be the first to start and operate the air compressor. Bill really enjoyed operating the machine. The DL&W also employed several high school and college students from the Waterville area and other communities. In addition to track work, I also helped my father with time sheets for about 60 men.

Gerrit Hyde, one of the gang from Waterville recalled the jack hammers by telling a humorous story about another member of the gang from Waterville, Bill McCartney.

…One time, McCartney threw this jack hammer up on his shoulder and started walking (quite a feat since it weighed almost a hundred pounds). Unfortunately, it was still hooked to the air compressor. The weight of the hammer against his hand depressed the trigger causing the hammer to operate. There was McCartney with the hammer operating on his shoulder, his hat jiggling off and his glasses hopping down his nose. Finally, someone shut down the compressor.

---

[110] Perrone, op. cit.

In those days there were no coffee breaks, no portable johns or separate drinking cups for the laborers. Commenting on the water bucket with the community cup, Hyde said: "The old guys would come to the bucket, spit out their tobacco and drink. I wasn't going to drink that water. About 11 o'clock I was ready to drink anything and that's when I decided to chew," he added.

However, on Schuyler Street there were bars on several intersections where the proprietors allowed us to use the restrooms. This often led to an extra couple of minutes 'delay' for a draft beer or soft drink. The orders from the section foreman and the assistant foreman, my brother Rocco, were as follows: "Go in to the men's room and come out fast!" I only remember one instance when someone refused to come out when ordered. A fellow from North Brookfield had a few beers and would not come out. He was fired. My father who liked stopping after work for a drink, firmly believed in 'Rule G'. I was probably told other railroad rules but that is the only rule I remember. 'Rule G' is one of the operating rules for all railroads, prohibiting the drinking of alcoholic beverages on the job. I did not know of my father ever violating that rule during working hours, but I know of some railroaders who did. On Schuyler Street it was violated sometimes, but fortunately it did not create any major problems.

Gerrit Hyde and Roderick Fuess told of a railroad gang member, Dee Jaquays, also from Waterville, who played the Hammond organ during noon hours in one of the bars on Schuyler

Street. "He would play about an hour and he was quite good," Hyde recalled. Hyde said that in the afternoons the freight train in the Yard would spot cars at various businesses – especially the West End Brewery. "Of course, we would get off the tracks and sit down. John Perrone, the Utica section foreman would say," 'OK boys-while you're resting – let's move that rail.' "It was a great experience. We worked hard and had great fun, particularly on the rainy days on Schuyler street when we spent time in the bars. This would give the boss disciplinary fits," Hyde added.

Memories of that summer over fifty years ago stay in my mind. Working so close to the homes on the Street was fun and every one got along so well with the residents who were mainly of Polish and German descent. On the corner of Court and Schuyler stood a business called the White Eagle Bakery, owned by Mr. Boneski.[111] I still remember the aroma of the bread and jelly doughnuts, one of my favorite pastries, being baked.

Becoming restless at the end of the summer, with thoughts of changing my plans for college, I walked from Court Street one noon hour to the federal building on Broad Street and started the Navy enlistment procedures.

When the project on Schuyler Street ended, we celebrated on the last day with a big poker game.

---

[111] Ibid.

Near the end of Schuyler Street in the vicinity of Oriskany Street, a tall green tower structure still stands. The tower, though no longer manned, was used to control the lights and bells at five separate grade crossings.

Long before the advent of gates lowered and raised at railroad crossings, there were crossing watchmen, assigned by the section foreman, that sat in shanties and lowered gates manually and also standing at the crossings holding a stop sign to halt traffic until the train would pass. I often view the concrete remnants of a shanty that was once located at White street in Waterville and remember gates lowered manually at a Clayville crossing in the mid 1930's. A relative of mine, Rocco Rotundo, was a crossing watchman for thirty years and his son, Felix, told me about of a crossing watchman who died while he was in his shanty on the corner of Noyes and Schuyler Street. The shanties were heated by pot bellied stoves that used coal and it was thought that he was overcome by carbon monoxide fumes.

RAILROAD DAYS 155

Rocco Rotundo
Crossing Watchman-Court and Schuyler -1953

Schuyler Street Tower – This fifteen foot tower erected in 1920, is being maintained by the Utica and Mohawk Valley Chapter of the NRHS, Inc. Tower man-Salvatore Battaglia controlled the signals and lights for five crossings. Photographer -Jim Armstrong. From an article by Joe Kelly. 1970. Reproduced with permission from Observer Dispatch, Utica, NY.

My nephew, Sal Battaglia, who worked for the DL&W and Erie-Lackawanna from 1969-1976 (and 1976-1983 for CONRAIL and CSX), had been a section hand before being assigned to sit in the tower and operate the levers that controlled the lights and bells at the grade crossings. He worked in the tower for several years.

And a wood/coal pot bellied stove heated the structure. Bill Baldock had the day shift and Battaglia worked nights. "I had to haul scuttles of coal up the tower. There were four levers that turned these lights on for four crossings that cross over Schuyler Street," Battaglia recalled. "The train would sound the bell in the tower when it was approaching Noyes Street. I would then turn on the lights for Noyes and Warren Streets. When I saw the engine pass by, I would then throw individual levers for Court, Warren and Noyes Streets. Another lever was for Columbia and Whitesboro Streets. Also, whenever the train came out of the Yard to go up onto the Blue Line (this line followed the old Erie Canal) by the old Dunlop Tire Co. (now Meelans), I would turn the lights on for Whitesboro Street."

The railroad always wanted the flagmen of the train to check traffic at the crossings, but the City of Utica wanted the tower manned.

Because of the automatic bells and lights, the tower is no longer necessary and still stands, unmanned, at the end of Schuyler Street. At present, a few members of the Utica & Mohawk Valley Chapter of the National Railway Historical Society maintain the tower.

Battaglia also recalled that when the bridge of a railroad burned in New Jersey, 100 car trains were re-routed over the Utica Division and traveled down Schuyler Street. He believes that this was before Conrail took over the Penn Central Railroad.

West End Brewery. F.X. Matt Co. is one of the few businesses that is still being served by the railroad.(NYS&W).

BUSINESSES ALONG THE DIVISION

Numerous businesses located along the Utica Division depended on freight trains to transport commodities such as coal, feed, feed ingredients, fertilizer, lumber, milk, scrap metal and waste paper. These included a wide assortment of companies such as canning factories, knitting mills, a bleachery, milk stations, paper mills, and several Grange League Federation (GLF) establishments.

By 1958, in the Utica Yard and in New Hartford, the DL&W RR served approximately fifty companies on the DL&W rails and on the former New York Ontario and Western RR tracks (the O&W) that had been acquired by the Lackawanna (*See page 195*).[112] At one time, the O&W tracks extended from the Canal Branch to Union Station in Utica, NY.

In addition to the customers on the former O&W, there were approximately thirty businesses serviced by the railroad on the Blue Line, which started at the end of Schuyler Street, and extended along the Old Erie Canal on Oriskany Boulevard for about two miles. "When the Blue Line was being built, home owners disapproved of the construction and the workers were

---

[112] Rocco Langone Files, DL&W Sketch of the Utica Yard with list of businesses served.1958.

fearful of attacks. Work had to be done at night and the tracks were built in sections off the worksite. They were then installed at night to avoid possible assault by the homeowners. Along the Blue Line from Yorkville to Erie Street, there were 16 different companies. On many days we took forty cars on to the Blue Line-- fewer in the summer. We averaged twelve cars a year. Many of the cars were loaded with coal for the Utica Knitting Mill and sometimes we would leave the coal cars right on the main track over night. The Mill would later move the cars with moving equipment into the sidetrack for unloading. There were five team tracks in the yard and I recall cars loaded with oranges on the team track being sold right off the boxcars.[113]

Some businesses served were on the Canal Branch and some were located near the yard office in the freight yard. The railroad serviced Abe Nathan Scrap Metal and Waste Paper Co., Foster Paper, Dunlop, and the West End (F.X. Matt Brewing Co.). The biggest customer was the Utica Knitting Mills.[114]

The Canal Branch extended south of Oswego Street under the arterial bridge in the vicinity of Burrstone Road to the old O&W main tracks by the ninth lock of the old Chenango Canal. The West shore of the New York Central was located there and the O&W and DL&W each had separate cross-over that crossed the West shore tracks.[115]

---

[113] George Perrone Interview, October 14, 2004 and March 31, 2005.
[114] Taber and Taber, op. cit. p. 319.
[115] George Perrone Interview, March 31, 2005.

RAILROAD DAYS

There were many coal dealers along the division selling anthracite blue coal for the DL&W Coal Company. "The Utica State Hospital in West Utica received four carloads of coffee every year," Perrone recalled.[116] There was a bleachery in Willowvale, a Standard Silk Mill and Leather Company in Chadwicks, and a knitting mill in Clayville. Many farmers depended on rail transportation to ship vegetables, hops, and livestock.

In the 1960's, the railroad constructed sidetracks in Sangerfield to serve Wickes Lumber (presently Curtis Lumber) and the livestock feed companies. For many years in Waterville, the Haxton Canning Factory canned peas, beans, and corn. Dorothy McConnell who grew up in the village recalled unloading box cars full of cardboard boxes and cans. The railroad shipped large quantities of coal to the canning factory to fuel the steam boiler. When Louis Gale and Son purchased the Haxton Canning Factory many remains of coal were still in the area of the old boiler house.[117]

William Doyle said that Jay Burton owned a coal yard in the 1940's located on the corner of Osborne Avenue and White Street. After World War II, Ward Bohner purchased the coal yard and also operated a corner store there. A fire destroyed it many years ago. "Roy Corbin worked for Jay Burton shoveling coal earning a dollar for every ton he shoveled, Doyle added. On the

---

[117] Edward Gale Telephone Interview, November 23, 2003.

corner of Putnam Street across from the Waterville Textile Mill (owned for many years by Harding and Jarman and later by Barclay Mills), freight trains delivered hoppers loaded with coal to these businesses. The textile mill shipped and received goods from the mill.

As mentioned in the chapter of the Farmer and the Railroad, there were many communities where milk stations were located.

There were knitting mills at Sherburne and Norwich. The Norwich Pharmacy (now owned by Proctor and Gamble) sat next to the railroad tracks n North Norwich. Gaines Dog Food and an animal rendering works had an animal rendering works were located in Sherburne. The headquarters of the Victory Chain Grocery Company also stood near the tracks in Norwich.

There are only thirteen businesses presently served by the New York Susquehanna and Western Railroad that now owns the old Utica Division. The F.X. Matt Brewing Company (West end Brewery) is the only former customer of the old DL&W RR and Erie-Lackawanna that is still serviced by the NYS&W RR.

RAILROAD DAYS 163

Lincoln Davies Coal Shed. c, 1940's. Photograph by Max Townsend

The Borden's Condensery, which was located off Osborne Avenue (South Street) in Waterville before the fire of 1945. Later became the Dairyman's League Milk Plant. (Now occupied by Automotives Collision). Post card collection of Doris McConnell

Ye Olde American Hotel-Waterville, NY. Where railroaders cashed their checks and socialized after a long day's work battling the elements.-Courtesy of Waterville Historical Society.

YE OLDE AMERICAN HOTEL

A hotel built in the 19th century vintage once stood on the south side of East Main Street in Waterville, NY. where now, part of a bank building and drive through are located in its place. The original name was the American Hotel. My family, friends, and countless others had known it as the *Ye Olde American Hotel*. This Colonial styled structure dated back to 1812. After my father took over Section 69 at North Brookfield, the hotel was to become a daily stop after work for "Pop."

Garrett's Grill, known earlier as *Chris' Grill*, also served as a stop for the railroaders. That grill was located near the eastern edge of Stewarts Shoppe driveway.

These railroad memories pertain mainly to the *Ye Olde American Hotel* owned by two great friends of my family, A. Charles Woodhouse and J. Frank Best. Best, who had moved from Utica, bought the hotel in 1946 from Woodhouse.

After World War II, under the proprietorship of Best, the large railroad gangs favored the hotel as a place to unwind after a day of hard work in the summer sun in the Nine Mile Swamp and other areas along the division. When payday arrived every two weeks, many in the extra gang headed for the *Ye Olde American* to cash their checks and drink some beer. The first draft beer always tasted the best and Utica Club and Fort Schuyler were the popular local draft beers, be it ale or lager. I think all of my family drank ale. In later years, "Pop" came in, sat down in the back room at the round table and ordered a shot, a glass of ale, and two packages of Camels. A pitch game or liar's poker and plenty of talk and joking followed. The bar was always crowded and noise and laughter filled the crowded bar and some of the men played card games in the back room for beer chips.

One of the main house rules kept women out of the bar. Though one always heard colorful language there, the proprietors required orderliness and few acts of rowdiness or fighting ever occurred. "Chuck" Woodhouse, and later Frank Best, "Cap" Hughes and Leo Zweifel were the familiar bartenders. After work, the men entered the front door and walked toward the bar located several steps past Charlie Dovi's hotel barber chair. Occasionally, my father and some others parked the car in the alley and entered the rear door to attract less attention. The roadmaster and railroaders from other departments often joined the group at the bar. C. R. Graham, the roadmaster, an assistant roadmaster, heavy equipment operators, welders, bridge gangs, mechanics, and those from Syracuse and other communities, often stayed over night at the hotel. Gerry Furner, a Waterville member of the extra gang and I vividly recall the happy times after work at the hotel. "The wives didn't always appreciate this and often called the hotel," Furner said. Some spent an extra amount of time there after work, which led to frequent answering of the telephone by the bartenders.

My father looked forward to socializing at the local pub. While living in Waterville, he especially frequented *Chris' Grill*. His favorite was the *Ye Olde American* that he frequented every evening after work. A firm believer in Rule G, he enforced the prohibition against drinking on the job, and to my knowledge never drank on the job while track work was being conducted. The track raising project on Schuyler Street in 1948 was a challenge as workers used the rest rooms in the many bars along the street. To my knowledge he never drank during working hours.

RAILROAD DAYS

The day after a night at the *Ye Olde American*, Pa sometimes used the term "hot box." In railroad jargon, a "hot box" is an overheated journal box[118] located in the wheel area of a railroad car. The term, though, did not always refer to railroad jargon. I heard my father use the expression to refer to a bad stomach as a result of a night of hard drinking railroaders hung over from the night before. I think my father, the foreman, may have also experienced a "hot box" once in a while. This did not prevent a productive day in raising track, removing and replacing ties or other track maintenance activities.

The Oneida National Bank purchased the *Ye Olde American Hotel*. After purchase, when the bank demolished the Hotel, Waterville lost what I thought to be a 19th century treasure of a bygone era.

At the same time, the Delaware Lackawanna Railroad merged with the Erie Railroad and created the Erie-Lackawanna Railway. It seems ironic that the old DL&W RR ended at about the same time as the historic *Ye Olde American* of downtown Waterville.

---

[118] A journal box is an enclosed area over the wheel containing lubricant to prevent overheating. of the wheels of railroad cars. Lubricant no longer necessary in modern railroad cars, since wheels equipped with roller bearings.

The Canal Branch. Freight cars of the NYS&W in the vicinity of the Schiedelman warehouse. This sidetrack extends south from Oswego Street in Utica under the Burrstone Road bridge in the area of the former Chenango Canal lock number nine. It eventually connects to the main track. Photo by author.

RAILROAD MEMORIES OF SOUTH UTICA

Eileen Ucekay of West Winfield grew up on Roosevelt Drive in Utica and her backyard was located at the junction of the DL&W and the West Shore Railroads. "The railroads were a part of our everyday life, she recalled. Our meals and bedtime curfews were in tune with whichever train was due at that time."

The Ontario and Western and DL&W crossed the West Shore tracks where separate crossovers were located.

RAILROAD DAYS

...We watched the engines evolve from coal burning to diesel. During World War II, we saw several troop trains a day going by. My sisters and I and our friends would all run to the end of our backyard and wave to the soldiers and sailors, and whoever else was on then train. (We thought it was part of our civic duty to do so). After the war, whenever there were any trains-with or without passengers, we continued to wave-even if it was just for the train crew.

Ucekay enjoyed walking on the rails.

..We loved to burst the tar bubbles in the ties. We could never figure out why there was so much broken colored glass all over until my father explained that many tramps or hoboes traveled the rails and they would throw their bottles on the tracks. These men of the rails would occasionally drop off the cars and ask my mother for food. Since we had the advantage of two railroads intersecting so closely, it was easy to climb over or under our fence and use them as a shortcut to the Addison-Miller swimming pool on York Street.. Walking the DL&W would bring us out under the old Burrstone Road bridge or using the West Shore to get us to Sunset Avenue. Many times we had to jump off onto the grass to avoid train traffic. Also, we would travel to French Road to a dairy store (now Chanatry's Store) that sold ice cream, by using the West Shore Railroad.

Ucekay explained how the DL&W separated a residential area of Seward Avenue and Roosevelt Drive from what is Divine Brothers. During WWII Italian prisoners of war were located where Divine Brothers are located. There was barbed wire and watch towers in the area, practically in her backyard. There were foxholes and bayonet dummies for the soldiers stationed there for training.

The Continental Can Co., Bendix Corporation, and Lucas Aircraft bordered the railroad. Ucekay recalled that there had been a train wreck behind her house but her parents wouldn't let her go outside and look.

...I can still remember the pushcart (track cars), the smell of smoke from the engines, the lonesome sound of the train whistle and the fun of seeming to be in another world when we were walking the tracks. We were never scared. Nor did we ever feel threatened. I can also remember the clickety-clack of the train cars, especially at night.[119]

---

[119] Eileen Ucekay letter dated February 23, 2005.

EPILOGUE

"Don't work so hard!" the Lithuanian old-timer, John Giedraitis, cautioned me. "These tracks will still be here a long time after we die." Old John was right. The freight trains still transport commodities to merchants every day along the division. It is no longer the DL&W or Erie-Lackawanna, but operates as the New York Susquehanna and Western Railroad with its main office in Cooperstown.

A freight diesel locomotive of the New York Susquehanna Railway Co.
Photo by Author

It has been a generation since the last of the immediate family worked the Erie-Lackawanna. A few years ago I had the opportunity to ride in the cab of a NYS&W Railway diesel locomotive and observe the numerous changes that have occurred along the Utica Division. There was no other traffic and with feelings of nostalgia, I observed the tracks where many days were spent toiling in the summer sun and wind and the snow of winter. Most of the passenger stations and freight houses are long gone. Most of the sidetracks or passing sidings have been removed. The trains continue to operate where my family and I and so many friends enjoyed being a part of the old "Delay, Linger and Wait." At present it runs only from Utica to Sangerfield serving eleven customers..

The train still travels the length of Schuyler Street at the maximum speed of eight miles an hour and as I rode along the line I saw the old green tower, now unmanned, but under the care of the Utica and Mohawk Valley Chapter of the National Railroad Historical Society. West End Brewery is still there but the old pubs along the street are long gone. I notice a sidetrack that my father's gang installed many years ago by the Dry Ice business on the corner of Oswego Street. The roadbed along the division utilizes crushed stone on the right of way and has a more attractive color- grayish white. The ashes fro m the coal of the old steam locomotive provided the black cinders for the roadbed. The black color of the roadbed is only a memory. The tall signal block towers no longer line the tracks. At Richfield Junction in Cassville, the wye and a small portion of the Richfield Springs branch are still intact. The station, the section gang tool house, and most of the sidetrack are gone. The old bridge over state route eight has been replaced.

All of the old milk stations have either been torn down, abandoned, being used for various businesses, or for storage. The G.L.F. (Grange League Federation) evolved into the Agway business. They also have disappeared, along with the section gang tool house that housed the motor car, the water tank, our favorite well, and the station at North Brookfield.

The station still stands at Earlville;. My father was section foreman in Earlville for two years from 1938-1940. Galena was the name of the station at North Norwich near the sauerkraut factory, a huge bridge that had been built over the tracks was removed several years ago. The Ontario and Western tracks used to parallel the DL&W tracks in the Norwich area. Since the DL&W had no coaling station at Norwich, it would purchase coal from the O&W. The bridge over Mitchell Street crossing has been taken down. When the bridge was there, the railroad cars were too high for the structure making it necessary for the DL&W to use the O&W tracks to Sheffields Milk Station where the cars would then cross to the DL&W tracks.[120] Also, in Norwich, the tower and the beautiful brick passenger station still stands.

In 2006 an unusual amount of rainfall washed out tracks below Sherburne, especially around Oxford and Robinson Mills at Brisbane. Following that damage there was little or no traffic below Sherburne since that date. Also there is no business for the railroad south of Sangerfield. The damage closed about forty miles of track between Sherburne and Chenango Forks.

Further damage occurred in June of 2013. A great amount of rainfall caused washouts adjacent to the Loomis Road crossing south of Sangerfield and very severe damage just south of the Earlville crossing.

In the fall of 2012, U. S. Senator Charles Schumer of New York announced that there would be $4.7 million in disaster aid available to repair damage to the railroad from Sherburne, NY to Chenango Forks, NY. The funding is from the Economic Development Administration awarded to the Chenango County Industrial Development Agency. Additional funds needed for the rehabilitation of the Earlville damage will be raised by New York State and from local sources. Construction is scheduled to commence between Earlville and Chenango Forks in late 2014.

---

[120] George Perrone, Interview of June 21, 2005.

RAILROAD DAYS

Riding over the division in the cab of the diesel locomotive a few years ago, my thoughts drifted back in time when I was in eighth grade and a favorite English teacher, Edna Gleason, assigned the class an essay assignment. I chose to write about my interest in trains and railroads and I ended my essay with the last two lines of the following verse:

> ...*Singing through the forests,*
> *Rattling over ridges,*
> *Shooting under arches,*
> *Rumbling over bridges,*
> *Whizzing through the mountains,*
> *Buzzing o'er the vale,--*
> *Bless me! This is pleasant,*
> *Riding on the Rail!* [121]

Though much has changed along the division, it is a pleasure to see that the trains still operate over most of the division (at least from Utica to Sangerfield where my family and I, and many friends once enjoyed being a part of the old Delaware Lackawanna and Western Railroad (and the Erie-Lackawanna Railway).

Perhaps our country will witness a resurrection of the significance and need for well maintained railroads, and the tremendous influence they have had on the United States of America.

---

[121] John Godfrey Saxe Rhyme of the Rail, 1840s

After a career of fifty-three years on the DL&W and Erie-Lackawanna, Louis Langone,Sr. retires in 1967 and hands snow and cinder shovel over to number one son, Rocco Langone, who succeeds as section foreman in Utica, section no. 71. Photograph by David Chernoff.

Date Nails. Until the late 1940's, the crossties had nails inserted in the center of the tie marking the year the ties were first used—about 1911.

Screw spike (top) that was common on the Richfield Springs branch and some required use of T-shaped wrench. Bottom shows common hooked-head or cut spike, invented in 1831 by Robert L. Stevens

APPENDIX

The Delaware Lackawanna & Western RR Co.

Roster of Section Foremen of the Utica Division[122]
January 1, 1944

Name	Section Number/Location
1. Joseph Biviano	67 Norwich
2. John Perrone	71 Utica
3. Rocco Tofalo	72 West Winfield
4. Fred Julian	70 Richfield Junction
5. Tony Villante	66 Greene
6. Louis Langone	69 North Brookfield
7. John Cursh	68 Sherburne\
8. Jerry Massago	70 Richfield Junction

---

[122] Chenango County Historical Society, Compiled from List Owned by Elmer Ingraham. Modified by this author.

LOUIS C. LANGONE

The Delaware Lackawanna & Western RR Co.
Roster of Track Laborers of the Utica Division
January 1, 1944

Name	Section Number & Location
1. Domenic Langone	70 Richfield Junction
2. Frank Biviano	67 Norwich
3. Dominic Raffaele	67 Norwich
4. Dominic Polo	72 West Winfield
5. Cecil Trask	72 West Winfield
6. Stefan Klch	72 West Winfield
7. Paul Massago	71 West Winfield
8. Silvestro Spasaro	67 Norwich
9. Albert Lee O'Brien	69 North Brookfield
10. Jerry Massago	71 Utica
11. Santo Fama	6 7 Norwich
12. Charlie Stringham	66 Greene
13. Albert Baranowski	71 Utica
14. Joseph Beratta	72 Richfield Junction
15. Charles Nolan	69 North Brookfield
16. Frank Langone	70 Richfield Junction
17. Carl Howell	66 Greene
18. Alson B. Brown	72 West Winfield
19. George J. Nicotera	70 Richfield Junction
20 Francis Birmingham	69 North Brookfield

RAILROAD DAYS

Roster of Track Laborers of the Utica Division (continued)

Name	Section Number & Location
21. Charles Angle	68 Sherburne
22. Henry Cittadino	70 Richfield Junction
23. A.J. Osowski	68 Sherburne
24 James Carson	66 Greene
25 Paul McGowan	66 Greene
26 Bernard Julian	70 Richfield Junction
27. Rocco Langone	70 Richfield Junction
28. Vosyl Lotoski	71 Utica
29. Oscar Boutwell	69 North Brookfield
30 Chester J. Cerminaro	71 Utica
31. John Salamida	71 Utica
32. Salvatore Beratta	70 Richfield Junction
33. Elmer Ingraham	67 Norwich
34. Thomas S. Cardillo	70 Richfield Junction
35. Arthur Roys	Extra Gang
36 John Giedraitis	69 North Brookfield
37. Joseph Cincotta	68 Sherburne
38. John Langone	69 North Brookfield
39. Louis Hoag	66 Greene
40 Frederick Roby	71 Utica
41. Earl Japhet	67 Norwich
42 Arlo E. Foster	68 Sherburne
43 Emilio Giudilli	71 Utica

Roster of Track Laborers of the Utica Division (continued)

Name	Section Number & Location
44. Harry Dunlap	66 Greene
45. Ernest Clemens	69 North Brookfield
46. Calvin Clemens	69 North Brookfield
47. Charles Furner	68 Sherburne

ADDITIONAL PHOTOGRAPHS

A passenger train with winged panels (for the streamline look) passes under the old route eight bridge in Cassville. Photograph by Theodore Jackson.

Richfield Junction (Cassville, NY). The junction of the main line of the Utica Division and Richfield Springs Branch. Most of the tracks, the depot, and water tank are gone. The author recalls passenger train delays there due to other train traffic. Courtesy of Town of Paris Historical Society.

RAILROAD DAYS 185

Donald Morgan and Duke at Paris Station in 1946. Former railroad station portrayed in background. Courtesy of Donald Morgan, Max Townsend, and John Taibi.

LOUIS C. LANGONE

Putnam Street crossing, circa 1890. The Waterville Station, freight house, the Buell Boot Co. (former Waterville Knitting Mill), and Scranton Coal Co. Yard . Built by Putnam family once, it served as the first railroad station in Waterville. Courtesy of Town of Marshall, Dorothy McConnell.

Mary Susan (Fanning) Langone and twin brother Robert Fanning wait on the platform of the Waterville depot for ride to Utica in 1947. (Haxton Canning Factory (now Louis J. Gale Feed and Fertilizer Co. is visible in distance). Photo by Dante Tranquille. Permission of Observer Dispatch, Utica, NY.

RAILROAD DAYS 187

Waterville Depot c.1920. Files of Steamtown NHS Archives. Courtesy of Richard McKnight, Curator.

Waterville Depot 1920. Files of Steamtown NHS Archives. Courtesy of Richard McKnight, Curator.

DL&W RR station South Street, West Winfield, c. 1910. The building was torn down in 1970. Collection of Greater Winfield Historical Society.

DL&WRR station, East Winfield, with water tank tower just east of Sale Road. Post Card collection of Greater Winfield Historical Society.

RAILROAD DAYS 189

Norwich, NY Depot, 2003. This fine looking brick structure is one of the few train stations still standing. Presently used by city of Norwich. Photo by author in 2005.

DL&W Watchman's Shanty on Merchant street in Oxford, NY. Inscription reads: "Presented to Oxford Historical Society by Willard Roney. Restored by James Hale. Dedicated August 27, 1988." Originally, shanties were located at Merchant, Main, and Water Streets. Photo by author in 2005.

LOUIS C. LANGONE

Diesel (Switcher) Yard Engine 428. Used for switching until 1960. Then went to Binghamton and was used as a passenger switcher. L-R. C. Smith, trainman, H. Williams, engineer, George Perrone, trainman, K. Zimmerman, conductor, and A. Clark, fireman. Information-Courtesy of Doug Ellison and photograph from collection of Henry Williams, Jr.

RAILROAD DAYS   191

Former Sitroux paper mill located near the old elementary school in Clayville, NY. Files of Town of Paris Historical Society.

Oxford Depot was constructed in 1914 replacing the old depot. After the last passenger train on the division, the building was acquired by the Village of Oxford, In 1993, the village signed a 99 year lease with the Oxford Historical Society. Files of Oxford Historical Society.

A World War II freight train transporting tanks in vicinity of Clayville, NY. Photograph by Max Townsend.

RAILROAD DAYS 193

World War II troop train in vicinity of Cassville, NY-1C.1948. Photograph by Ted Jackson.

Washout damage June 2006 at Robinson Mills near Brisbane, NY. Photograph by Doug Ellison.

Washout damage in 2013 above crossing in Earlville, NY. Photograph by author.

Washout damage in 2013 at Loomis Road crossing. Photograph by author.

Early 20th century track car with section men at North Brookfield toolhouse. Second from left is Howard Silliman, cousin of Muriel Burnham who provided photo from

BIBLIOGRAPHY

BOOKS

Armstrong, John H. The Railroad-What It Is, What It Does, Omaha: Simmons-Boardman Publishing Corp., 1977.
Botkin, B.A. and Harlow, Alvin F.(Ed). A Treasury of Railroad Folklore. NY: Crown Publishers, Inc., 1953
Clemens, Ernest, Come Walk With Me. West Edmeston:1979.
Drury, George H., The Train Watchers Guide to North American Railroads., Milwaukee, WI, 1984.
Gelwix, D. E. Letters From An Old Section Foreman to His Son,/Letter No. 4, Omaha, NE, Railway Educational Bureau, 1935. (Copyright D.C. Buell)
King, S. The Route of Phoebe Snow, a Story of DL&W RR, Elmira: Whitehall Mail Service.1974
Pugh, Fred. Days Along the Buckwheat and Dandelion. Brookfield, NY: Worden Press, 1984.
Reinhardt, R. Workin' On the Railroad, Palo Alto: American West Publishing Co.1970.
Taber, Thomas T. III. The Delaware Lackawanna and Western Railroad in the Nineteenth Century, 1828-1899, Published by Thomas T. Taber III, Muncy PA. 1977.
Taber, Thomas T. and Taber, Thomas T. III, the Delaware Lackawanna and Western Railroad in the Twentieth Century, Part I. Scranton: Steamtown Volunteer Association. 1980.
Tanney, D. (Ed.) Remembered Years, Brookfield Township Historical Society. Worden Press.1976.
Wickre, John, American Steam. NewYork: GalleryBooks, 1988.

PERIODICALS/PAMPHLETS

American Railroads, Their Growth and Development. The Association of American Railroads, Washington, D.C., 1960.

Hatley, S. "Delaware Otsego Story," Trains, January 1988.

Preston, Douglas, The Lackawanna in West Utica., Oneida County Historical Society, Occasional Paper 18.Tower Topics,
Utica and Mohawk Valley Chapter of the National Railway Historical Society Newsletter, September 1979
Milestones of Progress, A Brief History of the Brotherhood of Maintenance of Way Employees (Pamphlet), Detroit, 1969.
Utica Observer Dispatch, May 21 and July 11, 2004.
The Waterville Times, July 2, 1936.
Stephens, B. "The Susie-Q Saga," Trains, January 1998.

WORLD WIDE WEB

www.fremo.org/betrieb/timezone.htm. FREMO-7-4-2004
http://www..steamlocomotive.com/camelback/.2004
http://www.steamlocomotive.com/pacific.2004

AUDIOCASSETTE

Langone, Louis C. Sr. - October, 1977.

QUESTIONNAIRES/LETTERS

Hyde, Gerrit
McLean, Bruce
Sterling, Ellyn

INTERVIEWS\

Baldwin, Richard, Phone Interview.

Barnes, Pauline

Salvatore Battaglia.

Clemens, Ernest

Cooper, Adele, (Chernoff,) (Halligan)

Coughlin, John Sr.

Coughlin, John Jr.

Cross, Dana

Davis, Bess

Doyle, Jeanette

Doyle, William

Dundon, James

Dresser, Gordon

Fuess, Roderick

Furner, Gerald

Furner, Ronald

Gale, Edward, Phone Interview

Gallagher, John

Huxtable, Doris

Jackson, Theodore

Jasek, Anne, Phone Interview

Jones, Ronald, Personal Interview

Kaminski, Raymond

Langone, Louis C. Sr., Interview, October 1977

Langone, Louis M

Larkin, Esther

Luther, Edward

Masca, Robert

McConnell, Dorothy, Phone Interviews

McKie, Albertt

Neff, Lucien

Nichols, Roger

Pierson, George

Raffauf, Clarence

Rich, Walter
Robertson, David
Schoenlein, Charles
Townsend, Bruce
Warner, Worth
Welch, Richard
Whitehill, Trent
Wilber, Mark

INDEX

A

AMTRAK · 14

B

Binghamton · **iii, 2, 4, 24, 25, 26, 27, 30, 31, 36, 39, 51, 52, 74, 102, 112, 128, 137**
Blue Line · 55, 131, 157, 159
Bridgewater · 36, 37, 48, 79, 102, 125, 132, 138, 140, 143
Brisbane · 25, 43, 174

C

caboose · 29, 38, 39, 42, 122, 132
Canal Branch · x, 159, 160
Chadwicks · 25, 161
Chenango Forks · iii, 25, 29, 93, 137, 174
Clayville · 25, 30, 47, 48, 49, 73, 154, 161
Collins, Walter · 89, 90, 93, 117, 128
continuous welded rail · 13

E

Earlville, NY · 25, 49, 65, 102, 103, 173, 174
Erie-Lackawanna · 137

extra gang · v, 55, 65, 72, 83, 84, 85, 86, 118, 149, 165, 166

G

GLF · 52, 85, 100, 101, 102, 159
Graham, Cliggord · 54
Greene, NY · 12, 25, 84, 179, 180, 181, 182

H

hoboes · ii, 84, 85, 169
Hubbardsville, NY · 25, 48, 52, 60, 75, 77, 85, 94, 101, 128

J

Jackson, Theodore · viii, 26, 29, 128, 130
Julian, Fred · vi, 36, 50, 55, 94, 142, 179

K

Kohring Crane · 73

L

Langone, Louis M. · ix, vi, 28, 72
Langone, Louis Sr · v, 27, 36, 55, 85, 179
Langone, Rocco · v, 31, 159
Langone, Rocco (1868-1963) · vi, v, 46, 47, 142, 181

M

Masca, Robert · x, 30, 59, 73, 131, 150
Massag, Jerry · 31, 103, 132, 179, 180
Mexicans · ii, 85, 86
Millers Mills, NY · 135, 138

N

Negroes · 86
New Hartford, NY · 25, 26, 27, 43, 50, 55, 76, 119, 159
Nine Mile Swamp · ii, 145, 146, 147, 150, 165
North Brookfield, NY · xiii, 15, 25, 29, 34, 49, 50, 51, 54, 64, 73, 74, 75, 76, 77, 78, 89, 115, 117, 118, 119, 124, 147, 148, 152, 165, 173, 179, 180, 181, 182
Norwich, NY · 3, 25, 26, 41, 63, 71, 84, 96, 102, 128, 162, 173, 174, 179, 180, 181
NYS&W RR · x, 65, 66, 67, 70, 101, 162

O

Oxford, NY · viii, 25, 84, 174

P

Paris Station, NY · v, 24, 27, 28, 29, 33, 34, 129
Phoebe Snow · 4, 5, 16, 196
Poolville, NY · 25, 49, 86, 94, 145, 147

R

Railway Express Agency · 94

Richfield Junction · 4, 12, 24, 25, 29, 33, 36, 48, 55, 112, 128, 134, 136, 137, 143, 173, 179, 180, 181
Richfield Springs Branch · 4, 50, 173
Richfield Springs, NY · 2, 12, 24, 30, 36, 47, 79, 141, 143
Roster of Section Foremen · 179
Roster of Track Laborers · 180, 181, 182
Rule G · 152, 166

S

Sangerfield, NY · xiii, 30, 34, 35, 51, 63, 64, 77, 81, 84, 93, 101, 106, 111, 112, 113, 128, 130, 145, 146, 161, 172, 174, 175
Schuyler Street · viii, 149
section foreman · vi, ii, v, 30, 31, 36, 46, 47, 48, 50, 52, 54, 55, 56, 70, 79, 88, 94, 103, 104, 123, 125, 127, 131, 142, 152, 153, 154, 173
Signal Maintainer · vi, 9, 63, 96
South Columbia, NY · 131, 132, 138, 140

T

Tofalo, Rocco · 50, 142, 179

U

Utica, NY · iii, 1, 39, 105, 159

V

Vining, Guy · 89, 90

W

Washington Mills, NY · 3, 28
Waterville, NY · v, ix, vi, 1, 2, 3, 18, 25, 27, 28, 29, 31, 32, 33, 34, 49, 50, 54, 55, 57, 59, 66, 71, 72, 76, 78, 79, 86, 89, 90, 92, 93, 97, 101, 102, 104, 109, 110, 111, 112, 117, 128, 130, 131, 140, 151, 152, 154, 161, 162, 164, 166, 167, 197
West Utica, NY · 43, 149, 161, 197
West Winfield, NY · vii, 2, 50, 71, 132, 136, 138, 142, 143, 168, 179, 180
Western Union · 31, 51, 57, 91, 95

Y

Ye Olde American Hotel · viii, 164